Bored in Big Church:

Recollections of a Church Brat and Tattletale

By

By Dr. Julie Tacker Barrier

With Brianna Barrier Engeler

Dear Kathy,

Thank you joining our life group.

May God Bless you in the coming year!

Julie

xulon PRESS

ACKNOWLEDGEMENTS

Alexander Graham Bell, Marie Curie, and Albert Einstein were great thinkers and innovators in their time. My father, Ralph Murle Tacker, is an innovator extraordinaire. He is the king of the extreme makeover. Every time Ralph faced a setback in his life, he didn't become discouraged or reclusive, but instead looked to his Heavenly Father for his next move. When Dad suffered from bleeding ulcers in midlife, he sold his burgeoning business and ministered as a volunteer missionary. A brilliant artist, Ralph expressed his gratitude to God with pen and paintbrush. After a second blinding stroke, Dad lost his right field peripheral vision. So he took up pottery — three-dimensional art that he could shape with his hands. He mastered computer graphic design, penned profound poetry, and praised God through his artisan skills. He even shared Christ with little children by showing them the Potter who made them and shaped their young lives. When Dad has a setback, he doesn't ask God why. He simply asks, "What next, Father?" A mature spiritual father, Dad never questioned whether God loved him or guided his life's journey. He simply communed with Him and asked how to navigate the turns in the road. Do you know what I learned about my Heavenly Father from my earthly dad? Dad was never out of options. Neither is God. When the sky looks threatening and bleak, there's the Son behind the clouds. This book is for you, Dad.

Who is on your list of super-heroes? My *Wonder Woman* is named Wanda Tacker, the genteel daughter of a poor East Texas farmer. I call her Mama. Her five grandchildren call her "Cutie," a nickname she called *them* with when they emerged from the womb, red-faced and screaming. Why do I see my mother as a spiritual giant? Because somewhere along her daily journey, Mama disappeared and Jesus took her place. She didn't have an ideal childhood. Ma B and Pa B, her parents, divorced and remarried three times, and Mom suffered through the bloody battles of each passionate dissolution. Wanda was a stunning beauty, but she never thought of herself as beautiful. She never thought of herself at all. Ever since I was old enough to notice, Mom was laying her life down for those around her. Daily, quietly, constantly, she prayed, cooked, mended, and served. She prayed for others over the kitchen sink suds, during her daily jaunts around the neighborhood, and when insomnia took over her midnight hours. Cutie knows the Father and His heart beats through her veins. Mom's precious union with Him leaves a mystical aroma of myrrh — beautiful, humble, self-sacrificial, full of Kingdom power and life. Mama, your life inspired this story.

Tiger Lil, as my baby sister was aptly nicknamed, took life by storm. From day one, she made every day exciting and fun. Kathy is a walking party. Her clothes are stripy, sparkly, and stunning. Her shoe closet is the size of *Walmart*. But there is so much more to Kathy than her window dressing. Her heart is the size of Texas and her passion for kin and kids is legendary. The consummate hostess, she celebrates everything and everyone. No birthday, holiday, or anniversary is overlooked, because Kathy wants everyone to feel special. I admire my sister most for her deep prayer life. Kathy and Jesus are tight. She holds onto a prayer request like a bulldog, and doesn't rest until she hears the heavenly answer. "Her children arise and call her blessed; her husband also, and he praises her: 'Many women do noble things, but you surpass them all.'" Proverbs 31:8-9. Kathy, you always amaze me and make me smile. Remembering our fun brings me such pleasure.

My life story is joy-filled and remarkable because God gave me a remarkable family. I am truly blessed.

Dedication

Dedicated to my passionate, precious, pastor
husband, Roger, and my beautiful, brilliant,
godly girls, Brianna and Bronwyn. I am
truly blessed by your unconditional love,
encouragement and prayers.

The Charm Bracelet

"**B**atten down the hatches!" I was happily brushing my molars early one morning when I heard the jingle of the kitchen telephone. Hurriedly spitting out my Crest, I scurried to answer the call.

Helen, my mother-in-law, was on the other end, announcing her arrival the next morning for a surprise inspection (oops, I mean "visit"). I swallowed hard, in stark terror, imagining her appearance on our doorstep sporting her orthopedic wedges and flowered duffle bag. When she arrived, we greeted her with a salute and prayed that she would not look for the dust bunnies behind the fridge or find the hair in the bathroom sinks.

At our house, "spring cleaning" was postponed to be "summer overhaul." In September, we shut our closet doors and hoped no one could smell the mildew or Odor Eaters. Old socks and holey underwear happily resided in the corner dresser drawer next to a stripy woolen poncho from Matomoros that I had no intention of ever wearing. Indistinguishable kitchen implements crowded silverware drawers. I only cook TV dinners, so I have no earthly idea what to do with the three wire whisks Helen gave to me one Christmas. The oven was a haven for black molten chicken grease, but its aroma gave me hope that one day I might prepare gourmet meals without charring them to a crisp. Such was the state of my *House Beautiful*. Helen was a stickler for tidiness, and I did not want to disappoint.

In desperation, I placed a call to 1-800-GOT-JUNK and told them to bring a large trailer and a couple of HAZ-MAT suits. Two big burly boys with low-slung jeans appeared at my door an hour later. Dewey and Billy Bob looked around, swallowed hard, and gave us an estimate. Two truckloads later, we discovered we had a two-car garage and a walk-in closet. To call the Barriers "pack rats" was a gross understatement. But underneath the squalor of discarded *Golf Digests* and Barry Manilow cassettes, I uncovered a priceless treasure . . . a tiny gold charm bracelet.

All of a sudden, my mind filled with images of my eighth birthday party. I stood still for a moment, caught in the reverie. All of my life, I have run headlong from one project to the next, barely coming up for air. College was a marathon race of twenty hours a semester and a double major. High school was a blur of musicals, boyfriends, science fairs, and gym suits. Junior high raced by on a set of roller skates, flying past field trips, pimples, and braces. But childhood . . . well, childhood was a set of blank pages, a book unopened in my adult life. Each tiny charm on my bracelet was a window into my past.

A tiny piano medal caught my eye and reminded me of endless hours spent plinking the piano to the tick-tock of the metronome. No snickerdoodles or after-school cartoons were allowed until *practice time* was over. Each minute was painstakingly recorded on a chart made by my piano teacher. Sometimes when Bach was especially tedious, I pulled out my *Archie and Jughead* comic book from the piano bench and left the metronome running. My mother assumed I was poring over the musical score to the clicks, when in reality I was dying to find out if Archie was going to ask Veronica to go steady. Betty said "no." Reggie said "yes," and Jughead just wanted another piece of pie.

In spite of my futile attempts to circumvent daily piano practice, I won the coveted daily piano practice award three years running. Mrs. Nielson proudly presented me with a treble clef that adorned our mantle for many years. I was glad I could play "Git Along Little Doggies" without a hitch, and that I progressed from "Indian Drums" to "Moonlight Sonata."

I continued to examine my little bracelet. George McCaleb's ruby-red heart dangled proudly behind the piano charm. Tubby George was my second-grade fling. He scrawled a note between spelling words that said, "Will you marry me?" Mrs. Olson, our second grade teacher, nabbed the note, thinking George was secretly helping me to spell "hippopotamus." When she saw the marriage proposal, she quietly chuckled and handed me back George's unabashed declaration of devotion. That Friday afternoon after school, George handed me a blue plastic Easter egg. I twisted it open, and the ruby-red heart charm fell into my clammy palm. George giggled, pecked me on the cheek, and ran away. We decided not to tie the knot, but I kept the ruby heart just the same and attached it to my precious charm bracelet.

On the other side of George's heart charm was my perfect attendance pin from Sunday school. The Sunday before I started third grade, Mrs. Brumit marched Randy Phelps to the front of the classroom and announced he had won the coveted prize—the perfect attendance pin. He proudly stuck out his chest, and Mrs. Brumit pinned his award from Jesus to his freshly washed IZOD polo shirt. Applauding wildly, I had a revelation from the Almighty. When I looked at Randy's bespectacled face, for one brief shining moment I thought I saw a halo encircling his blonde buzz cut. I determined that morning that the next year I would stand before God, the angels, and the cheering crowd sporting that silver emblem on my gingham dress.

I spent that entire year focused on winning that pin. The blue and silver shield had "perfect attendance" emblazoned upon the front like a banner from heaven. In order to receive the coveted award, not only was I required to show up every Sunday on time without fail, I had to read the weekly Sunday school lesson and bring my offering envelope.

But "perfect attendance" wasn't an easy feat to perform. Three Sundays in November I hacked and sneezed all over Sandy French because I wasn't going to let the Asian flu keep me from my trophy. In April I puked twice in church after eating too many donut holes before the sermon started . . . or was I really sick? I can't be sure. After my breakfast preceded me, everyone looked a little green around the gills. Later, Debbie McCoy and Vicky Palmer contracted the virulent strain of gastrointestinal flu that I so graciously shared with the class. Undaunted, I came week after week after week after week. . . .

Twice, I almost lost the competition because of an errant offering envelope. One windy March Sunday, it fell out of my pocket and onto the pavement when I hopped out of our Pontiac. Sweet Mrs. Bentley saw the little white square under the car and returned it to me in the nick of time. The second envelope fiasco came one May Saturday night when I decided to hide it in my Bible between Nahum and Habakkuk. I hoped the fiery minor prophets would hold it fast until I arrived at class.

When Sunday School started, I frantically thumbed through the Bible pages, hoping to locate my nickel for Jesus. Where did it go? I scoured all of the "ah" prophets: Isaiah, Hosea, Ezra, Jeremiah, Jonah, Nehemiah, Zephaniah and Zechariah. My tithe was nowhere to be found. Suddenly I recalled a *Lucky Strike* commercial from the night before. The book had something to do with tobacco—no, it was *Habakkuk*. I found Habakkuk, placed my envelope in the offering plate, and breathed a sigh of relief. After twelve months of hard work, I reached my lofty goal and wore my heavenly treasure, my Baptist banner, with pride.

The last charm on my bracelet was a tiny gold tiara from Momma, given to me on my eighth birthday. We celebrated at Grandma Tacker's house. Grandma Moy's kitchen was reminiscent of a 1950s diner, complete with metal chairs, a Formica-topped table, and yellow walls. I expected her to deliver my cake on roller skates while Elvis crooned *Nothing but a Hound Dog* in the background. This was Granny's feeble attempt at relevance, even though we were already midway through the sixties and everything was tie-dyed.

Mom and Grandma decked out the kitchen with crepe-paper streamers, twisting them from the light fixture to the table to resemble a merry-go-round. Chuckles the clown (Mr. Tye from next door) entertained us with magic tricks. Finally, it was time for the important stuff: ice cream, cake, and presents. On a steamy July afternoon, seven chattering little girls stuffed their faces as they sat around Grandma Tacker's kitchen table. Ellie from next door was a semi-friend, invited by Grandma because she really didn't know my usual posse. Ellie was convenient, and Granny needed an extra guest. I didn't care; I just wanted the loot.

My sister and cousins were invited. Paula and Kim came all the way from Fort Worth because Grandma goaded their parents into driving them over. Uncle Paul owned a drug store, so my cousins were loaded (at least to my way of thinking). They were required to bring something more than the plastic top at the bottom of the Cracker Jack box. I cheerily unwrapped the pink Barbie suit that closely resembled Jackie Kennedy's inauguration outfit. This was high fashion at its best, probably worth two weeks' allowance. My little sister scribbled a card and gave me a Rock'em Sock'em Robot set that she fancied for Christmas. We knew who *really* wanted this priceless treasure, and it certainly wasn't me.

My three remaining birthday guests were Lana, Laura, and Debbie Whitten. Lana and Laura were my best buds. We never celebrated anything without each other. Debbie Whitten came because I knew she would trash me on the playground if I didn't invite her. Lana and Laura pitched in to buy an *Uncle Wiggly* game. We loved playing *Uncle Wiggly* because it took so long to finish the game that my gal pals could always weasel their way to stay at my house until dinner. Debbie gave me underwear. Go figure. As we sat around the table eating vanilla fudge cake and milk, Momma handed me a tiny pink satin box with a gold ribbon perched on top. The bejeweled crown was stunning. Though the glint was probably from rhinestones and gold plating, it was the most magnificent jewelry I had ever seen. I hugged my Momma tight until I couldn't breathe, and I heard her whisper, "You'll always be my little princess." And I was.

As I gazed upon the four charms on my charm bracelet, several thoughts flooded my mind. Two of the charms were hard-won: the piano charm and the perfect attendance pin. I think they embody the two passions that have consumed my life: my faith and my music. Although God did not need my perfect attendance to pave my way into glory, He saw a little heart that wanted to know Him and please Him, and He smiled. Mrs. Nielson did not need to be impressed by my piano playing, but when I looked into her eyes I knew she was proud of me. The other two charms given to me by Momma and George symbolize grace—undeserved favor and fervent love lavished upon a little girl when she least expected it.

The four little charms carry my past into my present, shaping my story and reminding me of God's love for a little girl, and His constant companionship throughout my life.

> *O LORD, you have examined my heart and know everything about me. You know when I sit down or stand up. You know my thoughts even when I'm far away. You see me when I travel and when I rest at home. You know everything I do. You know what I am going to say even before I say it, LORD. You go before me and follow me. You place your hand of blessing on my head. Such knowledge is too wonderful for me, too great for me to understand!* (Psalm 139:1–6 NLT)

For just a moment, picture God in your mind. Who do you think He is? Describe three or four of His characteristics here.

After reading this story, can you recall a time or two from your childhood when you recognized God's hand in your life? If so, write them down. What happened? What did you learn about God's character?

Read Psalm 139 once again. In your own words, what does it say about God's involvement in your life? Does it challenge the way you imagine Him to be? Please explain.

Bored in Big Church

W ho brought in the sheaves? I really wanted to know . . . passing time during "big church" was a bit of a challenge. If my posterior wiggled or squirmed too much, I got the "silent pinch" from Mom's left hand. My dad, on her other side, got the "silent elbow poke" when he drooled and snored through Leviticus.

I started attending church before the crust of the earth cooled. I remember chucking graham crackers at the nursery ladies before I could talk. Sweet Ethel Bentley, the sainted nursery director, nearly lost her Christianity after I tore apart every crib and rubber pacifier in the joint. I vaguely remember lobbing chocolate grenades from my overripe diaper. Some of my peewee cohorts are still in therapy after their early encounters with *moi*.

Unfortunately for Ethel and her compadres, our family never missed a Sunday at Cockrell Hill Baptist Church. We had our own pew and everything. God help the poor visitor who sat in our spot! Mom scrubbed my jelly-smeared face until it shone. Pressed and dressed, the Tacker brood piled in the car and sped three blocks down the street to the church parking lot. The only Sundays we missed were when my sister, Kathy, and I contracted the three biggie kiddie diseases: measles, mumps, and chicken pox. The one and only Sunday night service we ditched was the night *The Wizard of Oz* aired on television once a year.

When it was time for me to "graduate" into big church, the rejoicing was heard for miles around. Nursery workers and preschool teachers sang hymns of joy! I found some parts of big church fascinating and others a snorefest. The upside was watching the flowers jostle and dance around on our organist, Mrs. Bates' hat as she tore into a lively chorus of *Bringing in the Sheaves*. Because we had a clothesline, it occurred to me that bringing in the "sheets" inferred my mom's favorite saying, "Cleanliness is next to godliness."

But watching Mrs. Bates bounce to the beat was only half the fun. Melva Shofner, the sixty-something soprano in the choir, felt she had missed her calling as an opera star. No matter what piece the choir warbled, Melva stood out from the crowd with her painfully shrill high notes. Shy Patsy McCormick hung her head in humiliation, as if guilty by association. Still, Jim Palmer, the choir director, always pumped his arms with unmitigated gusto as he led the congregation in a rousing version of *How Tedious and Tasteless the Hours*. That's a real hymn!

The "welcome" of guests was a Sunday morning staple. Whenever Laney Johnson, the fiery young associate pastor, welcomed the bunch, he intimidated the visitors by cheerily bringing them to their feet to yell their names for the entire world to hear. Pastor Dubee was much more sedate. Visitors quietly sat in their spots while the rest of the congregation greeted them in hushed tones. Either way, we all got a gander at the newbies and hoped they'd hang around until Easter.

Next on the agenda was a "responsive reading" from a gold-embossed tome the size of a telephone book. The heavy hymnal was full of these congregational responsive readings. The pastor intoned a passage in a rather dramatic manner and we hollered back a Bible verse or an enthusiastic "Amen!" Thank God we were reading English... I couldn't yell as loudly in Latin. Responsive readings were the only part of the service where kids could talk out loud—a nice change of pace from sitting in stony silence on a hard wooden pew.

One Sunday morning, I was feeling particularly pesky and decided to keep chattering after the reading had concluded. I was on a roll. Apparently my banter was incredibly clever, because my sister, Kathy giggled 'til her tummy hurt. My mother was livid. She gave me "the look" that could curdle milk. I blithely ignored her withering glance. Mom subsequently tried finger-pointing, knee-slapping, and other subtle warnings, but I still never got the message.

Our church was pretty small, and the pastor was so distracted by my antics, he lost his place and dropped his notes. My fate was sealed. Daddy threw me over his shoulder like a sack of potatoes and stomped down the aisle, heading for the parking lot. As I was whisked away to certain judgment, I flailed my arms and pleaded with the ushers, "Pray for me!" They didn't. Daddy didn't "spare the rod" that day ... I couldn't sit down for a week.

The "special music" followed the reading, giving Melva a shining moment in the spotlight without the other choir members "bringing her down" (in her own words). "God gave me this song," she chirped. The rest of the congregation was thinking, "Please, dear God, make her give it back."

Some hymn lyrics she belted made no sense at all. Melva warbled, "Here I raise my Ebenezer." Who was he and how could she lift him? "That saved a wretch . . . " Retching, really? I thought that meant throwing up. I'm glad God saved me from that! I was also mystified by all the ". . . ation" words: *justification, sanctification, propitiation, fornication, playstation* . . . oops. That last one wasn't in the bunch. At the conclusion of every song, Melva decided to take the melody up an octave to a range that only dogs could hear. We stumbled out of church, deaf and disturbed by her performance.

'Passing the plate' was an essential part of the service the pastor never forgot. We knew he'd command us to "bring all the tithes into the storehouse." He slipped up one Sunday when he was groggy on cough medicine, and cried, "Bring ye all the tithes into the whorehouse." It was the biggest offering we had all year!

Pilfering from the velvet-covered offering plate was a temptation for my buddy, Donnie Scott. He could just imagine all the Double

Bubble and G. I. Joes those crisp dollar bills would buy. I, however, loved the offering time. Daddy taught me that everything belongs to God, so giving Him money was the least I could do. Offertory songs were cool because it was the only time one could hear the piano or organ unhindered by shrieking choir singers.

They allowed me to play the offertory song when I reached the age of ten! Mrs. Bates was my piano teacher and had great faith in me. I practiced for weeks. Sweaty-handed, I plunked my way through *I Surrender All* and played it without a hitch. God was merciful. It was a marker day in my young life.

On holidays, the youth pastor preached a children's sermon. He summoned all the little people under the age of ten to sit Indian-style on the carpeted stairs and listen to a Jesus puppet encouraging us to share our toys. I had trouble sharing my spot on the carpet . . . much less my worldly belongings. But I did feel mildly convicted about chopping off my little sister, Kathy's ponytail while she slept through the sermon one Sunday. So I repented in dust and ashes and apologized.

Pastor Dubee's sermons had a hypnotic effect. He could make any Bible passage sound boring. I called this phenomenon preaching with his "elevator voice." Laney was flashy and compelling. He started with a joke to loosen up the crowd and then proceeded to dramatize an exciting Bible story like Elijah calling fire down from heaven. I sat on the edge of my seat, mesmerized. Pastor Dubee soon changed professions and became a psychologist. Then only one person at a time had to be bored.

Pastor John Schwensen followed Pastor Dubee. He had a big, booming voice like James Earl Jones. I closed my eyes and imagined God Himself was speaking with that powerful baritone. Preschool bulletin-coloring turned into note-writing with my friends, which evolved into hand-holding with my boyfriends. In spite of my persistent efforts to avoid theology, many times the preacher stopped speaking and the Holy Spirit talked just to me. I looked around to see if anyone else heard the still, small voice I did. Then I knew, in my heart of hearts, God longed to have a relationship with me, His little child.

I have since heard that still, small voice comforting me and guiding my steps day-by-day. His is the call, the heart-song, the voice I love to hear above all others—my Shepherd, my Savior, my Friend.

I recall a Bible story about a young boy named Samuel who heard a whisper when he was quietly sleeping. Samuel assumed that the voice he heard was his mentor, Eli, the elderly priest. The wizened old teacher advised his little altar boy to say, "Speak Lord, your servant is listening," when he heard the voice again. Samuel heard God speak, and his life was forever transformed.

> *One night Eli, whose eyes were becoming so weak that*
> *he could barely see, was lying down in his usual place.*

The lamp of God had not yet gone out, and Samuel was lying down in the temple of the LORD, where the ark of God was. Then the LORD called Samuel. Samuel answered, "Here I am." And he ran to Eli and said, "Here I am; you called me." But Eli said, "I did not call; go back and lie down." So he went and lay down. Again the LORD called, "Samuel!" And Samuel got up and went to Eli and said, "Here I am; you called me." "My son," Eli said, "I did not call; go back and lie down." Now Samuel did not yet know the LORD: The word of the LORD had not yet been revealed to him. The LORD called Samuel a third time, and Samuel got up and went to Eli and said, "Here I am; you called me." Then Eli realized that the LORD was calling the boy. So Eli told Samuel, "Go and lie down, and if he calls you, say, 'Speak, LORD, for your servant is listening.'" So Samuel went and lay down in his place. The LORD came and stood there, calling as at the other times, "Samuel! Samuel!" Then Samuel said, "Speak, for your servant is listening." (1 Samuel 3:2–10 NIV)

Can you imagine a heavenly Father who longs to spend time communing with you, His precious child? What emotions do you feel in response? Do you believe that this is true? Why, or why not?

God wants to share His divine secrets with you. He longs to speak words of love to your heart. He eagerly waits for those moments you share when you come into His house to worship. Is going to church drudgery for you, or do you wait with eager anticipation to meet with God?

List some times in your life when the Holy Spirit touched your heart as you worshiped God. What happened? What did He say to you? How did He speak?

Pray for His voice to guide you. Quiet your heart today, and enjoy His presence.

Board Games

Becky and Vicky Palmer were the playmates from hell. Oh yes, they were from a sanctimonious church-going family, but suffice it to say, my parents were sure they were the spawn of Satan. We gathered weekly on Sunday evenings. The grownups played "forty-two" and the Palmer and Tacker girls were left to their own devices. My sister, Kathy and I got into so much trouble when the Palmer kids came to visit that Daddy spanked us both before they arrived as a precautionary measure. . . . That was an exercise in futility.

When we four little instigators entered a room, the mischief factor increased exponentially. We always blamed the disasters on Becky, the oldest Palmer. She was the mastermind. Vicky, her little sister, was the snitch. And, of course, my sister and I were blameless, without fault. The four of us attended Sunday school together that very morning. How degenerate could we become between lunch and dinner?

Mom instructed us to play quietly in our room. Becky showed us how to crawl out of the bedroom window. In addition to blatant disobedience of our parent's orders, we lost all sense of kindness and good sportsmanship. Like clockwork, World War III broke out in our room. Bedlam, destruction, and devastation ensued. The once charming cotton-candy pink bedroom looked like a war zone. Our parents pulled us apart, marched Becky and Vicky home, and grounded us for life. Three days later, my sister and I pleaded for Becky and Vicky to return.

What transpired when we were with our partners in crime? We became surly and rebellious. We believed our moms and dads had devolved into idiots. We obviously knew better than they did. The big sisters (Becky and I) would belittle the little sisters (Kathy and Vicky). Our little sisters would, in turn, become selfish and belligerent. Nobody shared. Barbie got her head shaved and Midge, her plastic buddy, ran around naked. Magic Marker found its way onto white socks and sheets. Books were thrown, juice was spilt, toys were strewn, and tattles-tailed. Havoc reigned.

Our parents, desperate for relief, decided to dig deep into their pocket books and invest in some "play therapy." The Palmer and Tacker parents couldn't afford a Sunday night baby-sitter, so they drove us down to *Toys 'R' Us* and gave us carte blanche to purchase five board games of our choice.

Board games are the biggest rip-off in toy history. Milton and Bradley are laughing their faces off all the way to the bank. Frazzled moms and dads shell out twenty dollars a pop for two sheets of cardboard, fifty tiny plastic pieces, and complicated instructions as long as the Constitution. I think board games were invented to help frazzled mothers and unimaginative baby-sitters prevent their antsy little charges from climbing the walls, raiding the lipstick drawer, or trying to flush Ken down the toilet.

One would think that board games designed to tease the brain and sharpen the reflexes with buzzers, buttons, and sand hour-glasses would improve a kid's intellect and physical prowess. However, after hours of racing, buzzing and splatting, every participant was trigger-happy and on his or her last nerve. Of course, Kathy and I took every opportunity to squash each other's ego by making every aspect of our day a competition. Who could suck down a bowl of *Captain Crunch* the fastest? Who could chug a *Dr. Pepper* down without taking a breath? Which sister could bathe and brush teeth in under three minutes? (Good hygiene was never our strong suit.) Who could scream so high and loud that only dogs could hear? (That game was always a tie.) Board games simply reinforced the need to dominate, diss, and destroy the opponent.

Monopoly has always been the parental game of choice. Feeding on the greed embedded in the heart of every kid, *Monopoly* was open-ended. You could play the game 'til the cows came home. The winners were drunk with power, and the losers were penniless and suicidal. I used to fantasize about stacking globs of red hotels on Park Place and swiping every dime from my gullible playmates.

My little sister, Kathy, liked to swallow the little green houses when no one was looking. She said they tasted like chicken. The severe housing shortage caused by Kathy's snack shacks forced Mommy to frantically plunk down another twenty for more *Monopoly* fun . . . so we could continue to "go to jail, go directly to jail" and embezzle municipal funds by pilfering "free parking" bucks.

I always let Dougie, my next-door neighbor, buy B. & O. Railroad because it provided me with an infinite number of one-liners about sweat or gas emanating from his odiferous little body. The longer we played, the meaner and greedier I got. A high-society *Monopoly* snob, I looked down my nose at the poor sap that owned Baltic Avenue and called him "trailer-trash." The blue-collar Water Works kid suffered my plumber insults about beer-bellies and low-hanging blue jeans. Mad and miserly, I grabbed the funny money away from my chums and left them homeless and dependent on donations from the community chest. *Monopoly* never ended well.

Sorry was another foray into the fine art of brow-beating and grudge-holding. I secretly delighted in making my playmates feel like worthless losers. I always got a huge rush from being judgmental. It came so naturally. I had no intention of saying "sorry" to anyone for any reason. By the time our game was over, no one was sorry about anything and everyone wanted to get even.

Twister was a hoot. Of course, the price of *Twister* was thirty dollars because it contained a little plastic rug and spinner. Who knows how many toy elves it took to spray-paint the circles on the plastic? *Twister* was all about domination. *Monopoly* made you greedy, *Sorry* made you sassy, and *Twister* made you mad. Every *Twister* tournament degenerated into tickle wars and fistfights. No game should place so many antagonistic little monsters in such close proximity and expect them not to violate their neighbor's personal space. Kathy was a shoe-in for *Twister* triumph. She was rubber-band flexible (she could suck her toes) and could contort her little body into a pretzel. Kathy was unstoppable. Her secret weapon was her plump little rear end. She knocked the competition senseless with a well-placed blow. *Twister* should never be attempted without adult supervision and a couple of straitjackets.

Operation was designed to teach anatomy, though large portions of the body were omitted for obvious reasons. This game squashed the dreams of would-be little surgeons because every time a player dropped a teensy body part, the patient died and they lost the game. So much for the *Hippocratic Oath*! The game of *Life* was a bummer for me because one wrong roll of the dice left me an unemployed college dropout while Kathy won a Porsche, a husband, and a set of twins.

Card playing was cheap but perilous. Nothing good could come of a deck with naked "Bicycle" ladies on the back of each heart, spade, and club. Card-playing was only for evil sinners. You might start out with *Go Fish*, but *Go Fish* led to *Gin Rummy*. *Gin Rummy* led to *Poker,* and *Poker* led to Vegas. . . .

Board games may have temporarily alleviated boredom in spunky, punchy little offspring, but in my estimation, Milton and Bradley and their buddies in the toy industry simply exploited every corrupt tendency in the heart of a child. The winners berated and bullied the losers, the losers retaliated with fury, and the quiet embezzlers hoarded their spoils. For my money, parents should have saved the cash and handed their little charges a box of Crayolas and some glue to sniff.

> *If you are wise and understand God's ways, live a life of steady goodness so that only good deeds will pour forth. And if you don't brag about the good you do, then you will be truly wise! But if you are bitterly jealous and there is selfish ambition in your hearts, don't brag about being wise. That is the worst kind of lie. For jealousy and selfishness are not God's kind of wisdom. Such things are earthly, unspiritual, and motivated by the Devil. For wherever there is jealousy and selfish ambition, there you will find disorder and every kind of evil. But the wisdom that comes from heaven is first of all pure. It is also peace loving, gentle at all times, and willing to yield to others. It is full of mercy and good deeds. It shows no partiality and is always sincere. And those who are peacemakers will plant seeds of peace and reap a harvest of goodness.*
> (James 3:13–4:1 NLT)

Sinful behavior destroys intimacy with God and others. Study James 3:13–18 above. James provides a compelling contrast between those who are driven by selfish ambition and those who humbly surrender to God's will. List the adjectives James uses in this passage, then write a sentence describing the difference between the two sides.

Can you think of a time when you exhibited selfish, unkind behavior? What happened?How did it make you feel? How did it destroy intimacy with those around you?

Remember a time when you walked in "heavenly wisdom" (3:17). Using the adjectives you listed for the first question, circle those that describe godly behavior. How can Christ-like behavior affect those around you?

Brainstorm at least three different actions you could take to humbly build others up around you instead of tearing them down with a competitive spirit. Which one will you put into practice this week?

Jibber-Jabber

I burst forth from my mother's womb with a bang. Mom screamed, placenta flew, and Daddy fainted. The doctor forgot to press the mute button when he spanked my shiny pink behind. I popped out bawling like a banshee (so I'm told), and I screamed non-stop for the first three months of my life. The pediatrician recommended that Mom lace my formula with Valium. Oh, wait . . . the valium was for *her.*

Daddy named me Julie because I entered the world on a sweltering day in July. He dubbed me Julie *Gail* because he instinctively knew I'd be full of hot air and would blow through life like a whirlwind.

Babies are blissfully unaware of two things. One, the world does not revolve around them, and two, the high-pitched sound emitted from their teeny-tiny vocal cords can break the sound barrier and send their parents to the loony bin. Poor Mom couldn't decide whether my persistent yelling was an insatiable desire to be cuddled and fed or if I simply loved the sound of my own voice. They never knew that the culprit—the source of my agony—was diaper rash. You see, when I was an infant in the days before the flood, *Pampers* were non-existent and central air-conditioning was a pipe dream. The only cooling for a muggy summer afternoon was a hamster wheel-powered fan blowing over a large ice cube (a bit of a hyperbole—but almost true). My bottom was raw, and I had no qualms about sharing my misery.

I found many causes for complaints in my young life. I felt there was a shocking lack of Gerber's banana pudding. I thought hard rubber pacifiers really sucked and the liars at *Johnson's Baby Shampoo* deceived me by promising that their shampoo guaranteed "no more tears." New parents of babies are oblivious to such indignities. Mom and Dad performed perfunctory rituals that included burping, bootie-tying, and booger-blowing. I tried to tell them that I really wanted more rocking, blubber-belly kissing, peek-a-boo playing, and toe tickling!

My toddler days were never quiet. One of my earliest childhood memories was my first attempt at singing. I happily swung my chubby baby feet while finger-painting my high chair tray with butterscotch pudding. Across the room, I spied an incredibly large lady singing *La Traviata* on the *Ed Sullivan Show*. The sound was mesmerizing. Suddenly, I had an epiphany. The booming, piercing, screeching soprano notes were filled with a shaky sound. I learned much later that good singers sing with vibrato. I didn't know what "vibrato" was, but I was willing to give it a shot. I threw my head back, kicked my feet to make the shaky sound and hit a pitch that only dogs could hear. Well, that's a bit of an exaggeration. Mom heard it loud and clear. She jumped up from the table, wincing and covering her ears. Slimy and butterscotch-brown, I was quickly banished to the playpen at the far end of the house. Apparently, my singing debut wouldn't land me a spot on *American Idol*.

The world was filled with wonderful words and sounds, and I wanted to sing and say all of them (except the naughty ones, of course). I chattered all the way through preschool. My classmates didn't seem to mind, but I heard my teacher tell my Mom I was "a bit of a handful." Is that why my naptime was twice as long as everyone else's? None of the other kids got to share their treasures at Show and Tell because I sprinted to the front of the class, waxed eloquent for ten minutes about my Twinkies and my goldfish Boo Boo without drawing a breath. Sydney Nettleworth didn't seem to mind. She was petrified to talk in public, even about Puffy her guinea pig or the magical corny dog she downed at *Der Wienerschnitzel*.

Elementary school rules placed unwelcome constraints on my motor-mouth. Every kindergarten child wistfully dreamt of laying aside Crayolas and play dough for a lunch box and a *Fun with Dick and Jane* reader. Some of my kindergarten cronies had apprehensions about the big brick box down the street that was L.O. Donald School, but not me. I was sure I would take the place by storm. After all, I already knew my *ABC's* and could tie the "Bunny ears" on my sneakers. Mom received the school supply list with the necessary items to begin my scholastic career: a pink eraser, lined paper, Elmer's glue, and of course, my number two pencil. I stared at my closet in a quandary: I had my jumper and sneakers, but how to accessorize? I badgered Mommy with questions. Do I have to wear a petticoat? Petticoats were hot and itchy. Would I have to carry a sweater? Sweaters were for babies and old people. Did I get a locker or a cubby? I wanted a locker like the big kids down the street. Mom shut me up by stuffing a fruit rollup in my mouth and sending me outside to play.

On the first day of school, the alarm clock buzzed and I shot out of bed like a rocket. Mommy and Daddy walked me to the bus, looking very relieved. We were herded to the blacktop in the school-yard, and Principal Moffett called out each name. We were to line up behind our teacher. "Julie Tacker," he said. "Here!" I chirped. "Mrs. Hubbard, Turtle Class."

Well, I was no idiot. Four classes of first graders huddled together: the Turtles, the Lambs, the Bunnies, and the Slugs. The Bunnies bounced, the Turtles crept, the Lambs dawdled, and the Slugs rode the short bus. My birthday was in July, so the powers that be assumed I was a "Turtle," a late-bloomer. I hated those Bunnies already. However, Mrs. Hubbard did seem nice. She had a shiny barrette in her hair and a striped dress that made her look like June Cleaver on "Leave It to Beaver."

Poor Mrs. Hubbard . . . she never saw it coming. The hurricane that was me blew into her once peaceful classroom. I ran around the room's perimeter at least three times to be sure I saw every bulletin board and eraser. I told everyone who'd listen that I had Fruit Loops for breakfast and that my favorite color was red. Then I moved on to important questions like, "When is recess?" and "Why do I have to sit behind Bobby Gibble? He always has gas." If Mrs. Hubbard had a question, my hand shot up like Sputnik and I blurted the answer. It didn't matter if I knew the answer or even heard the question. I still got to talk. After a few boring spelling words and a half hour of addition, the lunch bell finally rang. I grabbed my Barbie lunch box and bolted for the door. Mrs. Hubbard grabbed me by the nape of the neck and sentenced me to the back of the line. I guessed most of first grade would be spent in stony silence, waiting and standing in line. The Turtle life was not the life for me.

When we arrived at the lunchroom, I rattled on like a machine gun about *Howdy Doody*, Mr. Moffett, my little sister Kathy, the dog next door, and my yummy *Twinkies*. (I have since learned that the delicious cream filling is used to cement the solar panels on the Space Shuttle.) Mrs. Hubbard had finally had her fill of this little chatterbox. She sentenced me to solitary confinement with my nose in the corner. I had to stand, motionless and silent, by the water fountain for twenty-five more minutes. Oh, the scandal! Oh, the humiliation! Shamed on this, the day of all days, my first day of school! Shortly after, I was transferred to the Bunny class. They were a little more my speed.

I finally learned that every thought that enters my head should not immediately burst out of my mouth. However, my propensity for verbosity has not waned. In high school, my speech teacher put me on the debate team to shut me up. In college, I spent hours warbling in the practice room to four walls that did not complain if I sang too high, too loud, or too long.

I eventually married a preacher. He *really* likes to talk.

The proverbs of Solomon son of David, king of Israel: for attaining wisdom and discipline; for understanding words of insight; for acquiring a disciplined and prudent life, doing what is right and just and fair; for giving prudence to the simple, knowledge and discretion to the young—let the wise listen and add to their learning, and let the discerning get guidance—for understanding proverbs and parables, the sayings and riddles of the wise. The fear of the LORD is the beginning of knowledge, but fools despise wisdom and discipline. Listen, my son, to your father's instruction and do not forsake your mother's teaching. They will be a garland to grace your head and a chain to adorn your neck." (Proverbs 1:1–9 NIV)

The theme of the book of Proverbs involves the importance of listening to God and learning in humble submission. Read verses 1:1–9 again. What happens when we spend our lives foolishly dominating conversation?

What are the consequences if we fail to be still and listen to wise counsel? Are you willing to receive counsel from others? Please explain.

What does a wise and discerning person look like? List some lessons you have learned from godly advisors. Describe some counsel you refused to hear. What happened?

Bad-Hair Day

Permanent waves are a bad idea. They were a bad idea in the 1950s, and their toxic fumes are still poking holes in the ozone layer even as we speak.

My fine hair was always an enigma to my mother. I was semi-bald as a baby, able to sprout only a few scruffy tufts above my eyebrows. Mother tried her best to use hair gel to cement the wispy fringe to my forehead with a pink rosette barrette. I think she ended up resorting to super-glue. Mom tried bonnets to cover my splotchy scalp, but I'd rip those suckers off in a New York minute. In utter desperation, she decked me in a profusion of lace and eyelet so onlookers would stop calling me Ralph Jr. (My father was Ralph Sr.)

My dishwater blond follicles shyly began to spring up around the ripe old age of three. By that time, Mother had discovered "pixie cuts"—making it easy for her to stuff my head under the kitchen faucet, remove any leftover gum or unwanted debris, and towel dry my sparse locks in less than two minutes. I resembled an ivory elf.

Time passed. My long-awaited debut into first grade was just around the corner. My sparkly pink sneakers were perched upon the shelf, just waiting for the sandbox. My navy blue jumper was pressed and neatly hung on the bedroom door. I even had my number two pencil.

The August days dragged on and on. Most girls *glowed* instead of perspiring. Not me! God strategically placed all of my sweat ducts right at the scalp line. If I were the least bit nervous or overheated, I looked like I had been in the swimming pool. Oh, great! That meant that I would look like I had hit the sauna during recess. The first-grade boys would taunt me and my gal pals would tease me. How could I survive such embarrassment?

Mother knew instinctively that I needed a way for my curls to stand at attention no matter how damp my locks became. She was determined to make me look spiffy for the "Turtle" class, so she whisked me off to the corner beauty shop. *Supercuts* had not been invented yet. Most haircuts involved a bowl and a pair of pinking shears, but Mom plopped me down in the faux red leather chair.

Three middle-aged ladies swiveled me back and forth, contemplating the challenge. Mrs. Snedley, the shop owner, narrowed her eyes and said "Hmmm. . . ." She summoned Gladys, the shampoo girl, for a consultation. Finally they took Bling Yu away from the manicure table to get her take on the problem. They whispered under their breath, shook their heads, and scrutinized me like a lab rat.

By now, I started getting wiggly and whined to hop down and head for the Coke machine. But the powers that be had decided my fate. It was time for a permanent wave. Because my hair was so fine, Snedley and her cohorts decided to give me a "brush up." This permanent wave allowed the thinner hair on the sides of my head to coil tightly around my forehead and ears like Betty Boop. At the back of my head, they would "brush up" the longer, thicker strands so that I resembled Peter Rabbit.

Mom agreed to the plan, so Snedley and her crew got to work. They donned their Hasmat suits, choked me with a rubber cloak, and wrapped rings of cotton around my head—scaring me within an inch of my life if I wriggled even a little bit. What followed can only be described as "hair hurricane." Mountains of spindly cylinders were rolled in front of me. They looked like rubber fingers sprouting black spider legs. The threesome scored my scalp with pointy instruments as if they were planning to perform a lobotomy. By this time I was scared spitless. Nothing could have prepared me for the gruesome ritual that followed. Each row of hair was pulled so hard my eyes looked like slits cut into an overripe tomato. The rollers were secured with the black rubber antennae. The indignity of looking like I was infested with gummy worms paled in comparison to the unabated agony that ensued.

"This might sting a bit," Snedley warned. Everyone in Dallas would soon be suffocated by the stench of peroxide and ammonium thyglocolate. The mixture slowly fried my scalp. I shrieked in pain, but Mom simply patted my arm. I wanted to slug her. Water torture, the rack, and even bamboo shoots under the fingernails must be preferable alternatives to the forty-five minutes of hair hell I endured.

At long last, Mrs. Snedley returned to my perch. Thank God, the agony was over.

But no! More pain and suffering would ensue. Gladys grabbed me and shoved my rollered head down into the shampoo bowl, dousing me with boiling water . . . rubber wieners and all. Apparently, if you let the ammonium thyglocolate remain on your scalp, it will eat through your skin to your brain. Finally the rubber gloves came off, the plastic spindles disappeared, and my frizzy locks stood at attention. I still reeked of ammonia, but they assured me the smell would fade in a few weeks.

The "brush-up" made my head look pointy, but I didn't care one bit. I just wanted out of that chair. Perms were not a good look for me. Undaunted, Mother lifted me from my leather perch and grabbed my hand to head for home.

"See you in three months," Mrs. Snedley chirped.

You've got to be kidding. . . .

You made all the delicate, inner parts of my body and knit me together in my mother's womb. Thank you for making me so wonderfully complex! Your workmanship is marvelous—how well I know it. You watched me as I was being formed in utter seclusion, as I was woven together in the dark of the womb. You saw me before I was born. Every day of my life was recorded in your book. Every moment was laid out before a single day had passed. How precious are your thoughts about me, O God. They cannot be numbered! (Psalm 139:13–17 NLT)

Oh, the price women pay for beauty! Even the most attractive women have features they despise. But God, your Loving Creator, looks into your eyes and tells you that you are His best work—His masterpiece! What does it do to your heart to know that your Heavenly Father loves you just as you are?

Can you look in the mirror and give thanks for how He made you? Why, or why not?

Take some time to meditate upon God's love for you. Imagine that He had a canvas up in heaven, and before you were ever born, He painted your picture. You were His best work. No one can take your place. When you catch a glimpse of yourself in the mirror today, quote these words from Psalm 139: "I am fearfully and wonderfully made."

The Kissing Contest

*T**he story you are about to read is absolutely true. The names have not been changed to protect the guilty.*

P.E. was the bane of my existence. Even in first grade when the Bunny and Turtle classes marched to the gym, I was definitely the slug of the bunch. Dodge balls pelted me, tetherballs whacked me in the jaw, and soccer balls whizzed between my legs to the goal of the opposing team. When Marvin and Buddy, team captains, surveyed their potential teammates, I was the last girl standing. How humiliating! I had no physical impairment; I just excelled in *klutziness*.

Once third grade rolled around and folk dancing became our rainy-day curriculum, I finally found my niche. Clogging, hopping, and wiggling my hind end came naturally. Of course, rainy days came only once a month, so my classmates had little use for my talent to bust a move. I did have certain classroom skills. I could spell my socks off and captivate the crowd at Show and Tell.

Recess was particularly boring for a non-athlete. One could only hang upside-down on the monkey bars for so long. Swaying back and forth on the swing was iffy after lunch because I had just downed a Sloppy Joe filled with mystery meat and a plateful of canned peas. Tag was frustrating because my exercise regimen consisted of jogging back and forth from the couch to the refrigerator to retrieve Popsicles during *Pepsodent* commercials. Needless to say, my cardiovascular capacity was not so hot.

One sultry Monday afternoon, Diana Worthington, Tony Sirchia, George McCaleb, and I had an inspired idea. Why not have a kissing contest? Scientists call kissing *osculation*. Grandparents called it *spooning,* and parents call it *smooching*, Teenagers call it *suckus face-ikus*. I was not a stranger to the fine art of kissing. In fact, I got started at an early age.

I kissed the preacher's son. Okay, I admit it. We were five. We were in love. Pastor Allen poked his head into the family room, thinking we were watching *Magilla Gorilla* and found us lip-locked. Unruffled, he said, "Why don't you two play checkers or something?" I'm not sure I agreed. I thought kissing beat checkers by a mile. Mike and I had been sweethearts for eons . . . six days at least. It was time to take this relationship to the next level. For some unknown reason, our parents thought a summer wedding was a bit hasty. Killjoys. In retrospect, I believe they were right. Mike's twenty-five-cent allowance wouldn't allow us to live in the lap of luxury. After all, who would buy my snazzy *Tinker Bell* thermos and magic markers for kindergarten?

I was sure I could wipe out the competition in the school kissing challenge because I could hold my breath underwater for at least sixty seconds. I practiced pursing my lips for hours, sucking my *Melodica* harmonica while I watched Andy Taylor teach Opey how to fish. Tony Sirchia, my partner, was a shoe-in because he took trumpet lessons. Puckering and spitting were essential skills for playing a brass instrument and his spit wads always landed with amazing accuracy. Tony was a "never say die" kind of guy—he had the moxie to finish what he started.

Diana and George were definitely at a disadvantage. Diana had thin lips, and George was so pudgy he could hardly reach her face without falling over. Diana only joined the opposing team because I promised to split my *Slim Jims* with her after school. George was also iffy about competing because he was recovering from the trauma of a Thanksgiving family reunion. Kissing caused George to shudder because the obligatory whiskery cheek pecks he endured from Aunt Myrtle and Granny Opal were indelibly etched in his memory. The moment the biddies had entered his front door, the slimy encounters were inescapable. Nightmares of being trapped by musty, perfumed grannies and aunts filled his dreams. There was no escape. His well-meaning kin demanded kiddie-kissing at every family gathering. But George was no quitter. He overcame his night terrors; pretended Diana was his slobbery pug, Pixie, and steeled himself to pucker up.

I was certain Tony and I had the potential to master the fine art of smooching. News of our adventure sport traveled fast and a small knot of Bunny and Turtle class members gathered to watch the competition. The crowd hollered, "On your mark . . . get set . . . go!" We four drew a deep breath and smacked away. Kissing *this* boy was much more disgusting than I had anticipated. Tony had been shooting hoops earlier, so he had B.O. and smelled like salt. I was also surprised to learn that little boys don't brush their teeth as often as little girls. I was sure I tasted his leftover cheese goo from last night's *Hamburger Helper*. Beside the fact that tasting and smelling Tony was unappealing, kissing him was like playing tonsil hockey with a vacuum cleaner or touching my tongue to a flagpole on an icy day. This would not end well.

The cheering onlookers counted to thirty, chanting and clapping louder as we locked lips longer. I glanced at Diana and George out of the corner of my eye, and they looked as miserable as we did. However, neither couple wanted to call it quits and admit defeat.

By the time the crowd reached forty-five seconds, Principal Moffet threw open the hall window above us and leaned out so far we feared he would fall headlong onto the blacktop. I don't know where Mrs. Hubbard and Mrs. Chase were during recess. They had probably retreated to the safe confines of the teacher's lounge to down a couple of beers and watch *As the World Turns* before Social Studies.

Principal Moffet was not a happy camper. He stormed onto the playground, dispersed the saliva-thirsty mob, and had a few choice words to say to us before we tried to escape: "I am very disappointed in you." He spoke in measured tones to express the gravity of the situation. "I am letting you go this time, but limit your playground activities to tag and foursquare or I'll banish you to my office for a week!" Saddened by the prospect that my athletic prowess would not land me a spot in the school trophy case, I returned to the mediocrity of team sports and longed for square dance days.

My secret talent would go unnoticed and unappreciated until I married Mr. Right. Kissing my husband, Roger, was much more fun than smooching Tony Sirchia. Roger bathed and flossed regularly—definitely a plus. However, Roger and I did face a few kissing challenges. He is 6'2" and I am 5'2," so a stepladder is often involved. Early on, I also had to remember to remove my retainer!

All humans long for affection. Our desire to be held, cuddled, and hugged is expressed the moment we enter the world. We never outgrow the desire to be cherished.

> *Let him kiss me with the kisses of his mouth, for your love is more delightful than wine. Pleasing is the fragrance of your perfumes; your name is like perfume poured out. No wonder the maidens love you! Take me away with you*

— let us hurry! Let the king bring me into his chambers. We rejoice and delight in you; we will praise your love more than wine. (Song of Solomon 1:2–4 NIV)

God created the affection between a husband and wife to be holy, wonderful, and precious. Solomon's romantic poem painted a beautiful picture of romantic love between a husband and wife. How does this passage make you feel? List as many adjectives or descriptive words as you can.

Is it easy for you to be affectionate with your spouse or near ones? Why, or why not?

The passage also depicts the love Christ expressed for His bride, the church. How does it make you feel to know that God loves you so fully and intimately?

Spend some time meditating upon God's love for you. Let His love free you to give love to others.

The Alien
Loneliness Is Over-Rated

EEK! Pink and puffy, wet and wiggly, kicking and screaming, the alien invaded our home quite unannounced (or so I thought). The mother ship deposited "it" in our spare bedroom, and an endless array of grown-ups waited patiently to pay homage to the little interloper. As I peered into the room, a foul stench practically took my breath away. I gagged and escaped as fast as I could. I did notice, however, that Daddy had imprisoned the blubbering blob behind wooden bars. Thank God for that!

Two days later, I caught a glimpse of the noisy little creature. My vision was a bit blurry due to insomnia from the piercing shrieks that emerged from the room. The screeching never seemed to end – day or night. As I peered between the protective prison bars, I was shocked to discover a much smaller, balder version of myself – a "mini-me," if you will.

What was it doing here and why won't it leave? My three-year-old brain was in a quandary. Life as I knew it had begun to change. Mommy stopped cutting the crusts off my peanut-butter sandwiches. Clean underwear was no longer folded and placed on the corner of the bed. If I needed panties, I had to rummage through dresser drawers and find a clean pair myself. Bedtime stories became shorter (and faster, too). Where were my kind, happy parents? This mysterious little alien must have sapped their strength and infected them with a dread disease. They looked haggard and mean.

As I surveyed my surroundings, I noticed that the living room looked as if a Texas tornado had touched down and deposited debris everywhere. Newspapers, dirty laundry, empty *Rice Crispies* boxes and muddy shoes littered the floor. Nobody answered the telephone. I went for days without brushing my teeth, and I was allowed to watch TV 'til midnight. I confess I liked the perks, but I knew something was amiss. Would someone please tell me what is going on?

Finally, in a rare moment of quiet serenity, Daddy placed me in his lap and tried to explain. The alien was my little sister, Kathy. She had popped out of Mommy's tummy two weeks ago (that can't be right!) Pop also informed me that this hairless little person was here to stay. I was both put off and perplexed. Why was I not warned of this catastrophe earlier?

In retrospect, there were a few signs. Mommy and I had dutifully assumed the role of flower girl and bridesmaid in Ruth Moore's wedding just a few weeks earlier. As I flamboyantly tossed my rose petals, I looked back to notice that Mom was wearing an extremely large pink lace pup tent. Mom's burgeoning belly took up three-quarters of the wedding party snapshots. She scarfed most of the vanilla rosettes off the wedding cake before the bride and groom made it to the reception.

Mommy's lap had definitely disappeared, and she also seemed crankier than usual. We often ate *Cream of Wheat* for dinner instead of meat loaf and mashed potatoes. Raiding the cupboard was always a treat for me. I was cuckoo for *Cocoa Puffs*! Another change duly noted was a sunny yellow empty room filling up with teddy bears and rattles I wasn't allowed to touch. Somewhere along the line, nobody was snapping *Polaroids* of every adorable antic I performed. My paparazzi disappeared.

I wanted to be the only kid in the Tacker house. My next-door neighbor, Dougie Scott, gave me a few tips on how to stop the insanity. When his howling baby brother Donnie encroached on his peace and quiet, Dougie duct-taped little Donnie's mouth to silence the howling. Dougie will finish his time out in 2040. My resourceful pal also tried bribery to silence the little intruder. Every ten minutes, Dougie coated Donnie's pacifier with melted *Fudgesicle* juice. His inspired plan worked like a charm…until he ran out of *Fudgesicles*. Dire times required drastic measures. Dougie hoisted little Donnie out of the crib with a Pooh bear baby blanket and hid him in the backyard doghouse with his pooch, Spud. Shortly after, Dougie was shipped off to Grandma's for a month.

Lana Rouse, my bestest buddy, gave me the low-down on ruling the roost after a newbie had entered the picture at her house. Her baby sister, Bitsy, had turned the Rouse house on its ear. Bitsy slobbered and gnawed on Lana's favorite dollies, dismembered her My Little Pony, and ripped every page out of *Good Night Moon*. Lana packed her Bambi backpack, stormed out the back door, and ran away from home. She appeared on my doorstep, begging for asylum. After three days, her mom finally noticed that Lana was gone.

This baby sister of mine had better watch out! I was not without resources. Armed with the advice of my cronies, I nabbed the little blue bear from her crib and tried to flush it down the toilet. Water poured out of the bowl onto the tile and into the hall. Spanking ensued, and the bear emerged from the dryer unscathed. I hid Kathy's baby bottle under the living room pillow cushion, and Daddy tanned my hide. My plots became more and more elaborate. In desperation, I smeared poopy diaper on the crib bars and cried, "The baby did it." My folks were unconvinced, and my *Jell-O* dessert was history. My last attempt to create havoc was to decorate her nursery walls with neon crayons and to blame it on my sissy. Nobody was fooled. My fury turned into quiet resignation.

Then one sunny afternoon, a miracle happened. I peered over the crib rail and baby sister reached her chubby arms toward me. She wasn't crying, she was cooing, and seemed genuinely glad to see me. Mom entered the room and perched me on a rocker cushion. She shoved a pile of blankets in my lap, and told me to sit very, very still. My heart warmed. Maybe this little person wouldn't be so bad to live with after all. Perhaps we could coexist peacefully. I still wasn't sure she liked me, because Daddy said babies often smiled when they had gas. But gassy or not, we bonded.

Eventually she stopped screaming and started talking. Kathy scooted around the house in her Hello Kitty pajamas and found everything I did to be incredibly clever. Peek-a-boo and hide 'n seek became daily activities. Sometimes she even grabbed a toy in her little fist and handed it to me. I also discovered why God gave Daddy two knees. One knee was available for each of us when bedtime stories were read. *Candyland* was much more fun with two players, and most of the time, Kathy let me win!

Life was good. We had the occasional tiff ending in tears and forced separation. Having a sister brought much more creativity when devising mischief. Kathy gazed at me with adoring glances when I wasn't supposed to be looking, and she was warm and cuddly on winter nights.

All in all, I believe the alien visitation to the Tacker home was not a catastrophe, but a gift from heaven.

Lone Rangers are just that: lonely. Frank and ferocious, Saul of Tarsus epitomized the self-made Pharisee. Like 007, he traversed his homeland, brutally exterminating Christians like bugs. Until Jesus got his attention, Saul needed no one and nothing. Jesus appeared to the arrogant lawyer, blinded him, and forced him to be rescued by Ananias, one of the very Christian "heretics" he sought to slaughter.

(Acts 9:1-17). Even after his shocking conversion, Paul learned (the hard way) that he didn't need to fly solo through life.

Just like Paul, the crusty apostle, I am a slow learner when it comes to living in community with others. It took years for Paul to shed his self-made skin. Salty Paul never minced words. The apostle talked tough. "Hand the sinner over to Satan until he repents!" (1 Corinthians 5:5) "If you don't work, you don't eat!" (2 Thessalonians 3:10) But Paul had a gooey center. He loved young Timothy and called him his " true son in the faith." (1 Timothy 1:2). He thanked God for his kind Brother Titus, and taught him how to shepherd a flock. (Titus 1:1) A gentler and wiser Paul wrote the Thessalonian church and penned these words: "Just as a nursing mother cares for her children, so we cared for you. Because we loved you so much, we were delighted to share with you not only the gospel of God but our lives as well." (1 Thessalonians 2:7-8)

From terminator to nursing mother? What a transformation! In the same sentence where Paul penned the legendary words, "I can do all things through Christ who strengthens me," he followed those famous words with, "I don't mean that your help didn't mean a lot to me—it did. It was a beautiful thing that you came alongside me in my troubles." (Philippians 4:13-14) Barnabas and Silas were his traveling companions, and even little John Mark, the screw-up too timid to travel, became his beloved friend.

Those of us who pride ourselves on our independence should reconsider. We need our "brothers and sisters" in the Lord. They pray for us, protect us, support us, and well, just make life richer and more fun!

> *"For I can do everything through Christ, who gives me strength. Even so, you have done well to share with me in my present difficulty."* (Philippians 4:13-14) *NLT*

Why could Paul juxtapose his declaration of doing anything through Christ with the thought that he needed his friends? How do faith and fellowship mix? Is it spiritual to "need each other"?

Who are the people in your life who have supported you in difficulties? Write them here. Now meditate on those moments of support and comfort. Thank God for those "burden bearers" who have come alongside you.

Ask God to open your eyes today to see people who are often overlooked. Perhaps it is the cashier at the grocery store, the shy accountant in his office cubicle. Perhaps it is someone who seems sad and depressed. Speak a word of kindness and encouragement to them.

The Retaining Wall

What do you get when you add a pound of double chocolate fudge cake, three liters of soda pop, fifty Twizzlers, thirty-two Zagnut bars, and ten little girls in flannel pajamas? The end of civilization as we know it. I had hounded my mother for a birthday slumber party since I was five. She steadfastly refused, in spite of my pleas and protests.

Mom threw zoo birthday parties, Disney parties, scavenger hunts, and masquerade balls, but nothing satisfied. Those celebrations were "baby stuff." A slumber party was a rite of passage for me. Staying up all night, giggling in a sugar coma couldn't be surpassed. After I promised to clean my room until Jesus came back, Mom caved.

A month before, I started creating my guest list. Kay and Kandy Oliphant, the evil twins, were must-haves at any social event. They were at the top of the class pecking order because they could knock a softball from here to China. Never mind that their bat-slinging cost

Debra Whitten two incisors and a molar, the Oliphants were cool. Even Mrs. Perkins, our teacher, snapped to attention when the twins rolled into class.

My next guest was Susie Netherton. Susie had scraggly dish-water blond hair, mottled freckles peppering her sunken cheeks, and buckteeth. I invited her because I wanted to be the prettiest girl in the room. No one would steal my thunder! Diana Hornsby and Becky Moore were shoe-ins because they knew clever party tricks. Diana had a lazy eye, but she could blow milk through her nose. Becky could curl her tongue and stand on her head for five minutes straight.

Sara Clack was the richest girl in our neighborhood. Her dentist dad Arthur bopped around town in an ebony *Lincoln Continental* sporting ostentatious *Armani* suits (except when he had some poor schmuck's slobber dripping off of his white dentist coat). Sara *had* to buy me a pricey present to keep up her image. However, since Sara was obviously slumming to come to my soiree, I was afraid she'd stiff me and wrap up some dental floss and mouthwash. I took my chances and invited her anyway.

Nancy, Betsy and Cherie rounded out the guest list. They had no unique skills, but they were great followers. Whatever scheme the Oliphants devised, the three stooges followed whole-heartedly.

Mom spent the day before in fervent prayer, baking cookies intermittently. I noticed knick-knacks disappearing from coffee tables and closet doors being mysteriously locked. She was pre-paring for the siege.

To my mom's chagrin, the magic night arrived. My friends stampeded through the front door en masse, trampling my dachshund Beauford and trashing the living room with candy wrappers. Becky Moore chugged down an entire liter of Coca-Cola and proceeded to burp the alphabet for her cheering fans. M & M's littered the kitchen linoleum and lighted birthday candles were tied to my poodle Hubert's tail. The cake Mom so carefully baked became food fight fodder. Mom found Diana Hornsby tied to a tree in her underwear. These antics all transpired in the first fifteen minutes. Soon after, the Oliphant twins got creative and stuffed Betsy and Nancy in the trash can by the street to see how fast they could roll the metal cylinder down to the bottom of the hill. Betsy threw up and Nancy popped out screaming bloody murder. The bedlam that ensued was not pretty. I ripped my best pair of cotton underwear due to repeated wedgies by twin number one. Beauford had a coronary because twin two chased him incessantly and set his tail on fire. Susie quietly skulked to the corner after being mercilessly teased about her overbite.

Mom found my father in a vegetative state with a remote in one hand and some Valium in the other. He was worthless as a chaperone. Every now and then he emerged from his man-cave to lick the icing off of the spatula, and then he returned to his peaceful hideout. Although she longed to join him and let the chips fall where they may, some semblance of order must be kept. She steeled herself for the task. Mom had bought a megaphone for crowd control, just in case things got out of hand. Big mistake. Kay Oliphant grabbed the horn and broadcasted the latest school gossip to our peacefully sleeping neighbors. It was ten-thirty…only eight long hours to go.

I never got to open my presents. My poor mother tried distracting the mob with "planned activities" like piñata pounding and *Pin the Tail on the Donkey*. Of course, the crepe-paper piñata was ignored, but Kandy used the pole to bust Budgie, our parakeet, out of his cage. Feathers and fur flew as Hubert finally got his shot at eating Budgie. The bloodthirsty mob cheered Hubert on in his quest to eat poor Budgie. Mom found Dad's fishing net and rescued Budgie in the nick of time. Poor Susie Netherton got her tail pinned instead of the cardboard donkey. Finally mousey little Susie retaliated by skewering Kay, twin two, with a well-deserved tail-prick. Anarchy prevailed. The only partygoer who managed to keep her cool during the fiasco was Sara. She would not stoop to such moronic behavior. Finally, Mom had an ally. She bribed Sara with a *Rice Krispie* treat to retrieve the megaphone and bar the door. The madness subsided…for twenty minutes. By eleven, the natives were restless. Dad emerged from his cave long enough to turn out the lights. Surely ten-year-old girls would get sleepy in the dark. Yeah, right! The cover of darkness only fueled the fire.

The clincher was our march to the retaining wall. This single event would cause my mother to ban slumber parties from our home forever. My little sister, Kathy, always hated me for it. The retaining wall of doom encircled my backyard. Towering nine feet above the patio, the concrete fortress just begged to be scaled. The Oliphants fancied themselves to be tightrope walkers, daring the rest of us to follow suit. Not to be outdone by the ringleaders, we all climbed the wall and dangled our toes over the precipice. Before Mom could blink, we lined up like Indians on the warpath, screaming and inching our way across the concrete ledge. The view was breathtaking — grass and sidewalk below, a full moon above, and my Mother calling 911.

At precisely 1:00 a.m., the parents arrived to retrieve their malevolent children and the festivities ground to a halt. Monday, when I entered gym class, my slumber party attendees treated me like a leper.

All because of the retaining wall.

I would never know the ecstasy of watching the sunrise with my pals, bleary-eyed and hung-over from eating cookie dough. I'd never know the sheer delight of terrorizing my little sister in the middle of the night with a can of shaving cream and a rubber spider. I'd never experience giggling in the dark, telling scary stories.

My life was over...All because of the retaining wall.

I did learn one life lesson from the slumber party catastrophe. I learned who my true friends were. Susie, plain and shy, turned out to be a faithful buddy. She never spoke of that fateful night. Susie made a place for me at the lunch table, shared her potato chips, and laughed at my jokes. Susie always listened when I talked. And when I was nicknamed "Party-Pooper" all the way through middle school, I'd cry on Susie's shoulder. And she would cry, too.

"Do not be misled. Bad company corrupts good character." (1 Corinthians 15:33)

Have you ever befriended someone who led you down the wrong path? Who was he or she? Did you know when you made the friendship that it would be toxic for you? Why?

What are some character qualities that you consider to be *good*? List them here. How can you cultivate them?

Who are your role models? Why do you admire them? Do you have people in your life who energize and inspire you? Ask God to lead you to some mentors and encouragers.

Geewhizzicuzz And Wallygoppers: Grandpas Are God's Gift

Grandfathers come in all shapes and sizes. *Santa Claus Grandpa* is a bearded, roly-poly bear-hugger who bursts into belly laughs at a moment's notice. *Santa Gramps* has an endless supply of Tootsie Rolls and puzzles. *Praying Mantis Grandpa* is stick-like skinny, with a shock of white hair and breath that smells of snuff and peppermints. He warns his young uns in a gravely voice not to sit on the plastic-covered sofa in the parlor—which is *grandpa-speak* for living room. Every now and then, Praying Mantis Grandpa pulls a Werthers out of his vest pocket and presumes he has just made your day. *Hippie Grandpa* still thinks it is 1960. He sports a leather vest and chaps, a perspiration-filled bandana, and a bushy beard. *Hippie Grandpa* roars up the driveway in his Harley with Johnny Cash blaring on his eight-track tape deck. Bathing for *Hippie Grandpa* is optional, and he often reeks of "oddly sweet" tobacco. It's a rush to ride his bike, but he often forgets your birthday. *Colonel*

Sanders Grandpa usually lives south of the Mason-Dixon Line. He comes replete with a drawl, a large glass of sweet tea, a fly swatter, and an endless supply of sweater vests. *Colonel Sanders Grandpa* uses words like *veranda, chiggers* and *Lamby-Pie*. He often resides in an oversized wooden rocker and offers a pudgy lap perfect for afternoon snoozes.

I had a super-hero Grandpa. On the 'Grandpa Scale' from one to ten, Grandpa Boy was an eleven. My grandpa could beat up Santa Claus, Mantis, Hippie and Sanders with one hand tied behind his back. His name was Ralph Waldo, so we nicknamed him *Boy* for short. Boy had sparkling brown bug-eyes, wispy, baby-thin hair, and a booming bass voice like James Earl Jones. Batman and Superman were "wusses" compared to my Grandpappy. Boy looked the other way when we bounced on the bed and never made us use our "inside" voices. He picked my hard-to-reach boogers without flinching. Boy popped his false teeth in and out (he called 'em "choppers" just to make us smile).

But Boy was no goofball. A mid-shipman in World War I, he guided a skiff that carried President Woodrow Wilson across the English Channel in the dead of night. Besides being a gritty sailor, Grandpa Boy tooted one of the original sousaphones in John Phillip Sousa's band. A sousaphone resembled a spittoon with a mouthpiece and bellowed like a cow in heat.

Boy chortled and told us Sousa asked him to play sousaphone because he had more hot air than the other band members. Boy used his lungpower to bellow the bass part in the church choir as well, and he taught my sister and me to sing as soon as we could chirp.

Boy and Moy (grandparent-names that were pretty silly as nicknames go) were powerhouses. The pair made the *Energizer Bunny* look lazy. After the war, Boy bought a gas station replete with ice-cold Coke and beef jerky. When pumping petrol and mixing it up with the truckers became too taxing, Boy semi-retired and spent the next thirty years selling real estate and teaching Sunday School. Gramps taught us bridge and poker. Good Baptists were not supposed to play cards, but Boy's years in the Navy caused him to bend the rules on occasion. Kathy and I could *royal flush* and *full house* before we finished elementary school. If we were short on milk money or craved an extra ice cream square, we pulled out our *Bicycle* playing cards, shuffled and dealt, and collected our winnings. Piece of cake. The schmucks that fell prey to our mean card shark skills learned to play and pay.

Nobody knew me like Gramps. I've been told I started shaking my booty to rock 'n roll before I could talk, and Boy assumed my fondness for shimmying and jiggling to the radio meant I had musical talent. He purchased a toy piano and showed me how to tinkle the ivories with my chubby index fingers. Mom and Dad were annoyed with my endless hammering away, but Boy just smiled and nodded. Somehow, he knew I had an undiscovered passion for all things musical.

Grandpa had a bum hip from the war, so getting around wasn't easy. He had a toilet mounted on a wooden platform and arm rails installed to make "doing his business" easier. For the grandkids, the potty platform was a magical place. We called it the "Throne Room," and the bossiest grandkid (usually me) was dubbed Queen. I sported a *Burger King* crown, a plastic ruler scepter, and a bed sheet cape. Keeping my royal robes out of the potty water was quite a challenge.

On my queen days, I perched on the porcelain throne, banishing my little sister, Kathy, and my cousins, Paula and Kim, to the bathtub dungeon. I was "Queen of everything" and Kathy was "Duke of not so much." She was forced to wear Boy's old suit coat and a mustache made of eyeliner. Kathy, Paula and Kim clomped around in Boy's size twelve wingtips and begrudgingly bowed and scraped before their queen. After an hour or so, I tired of being a tyrant and we retired to the bedchamber to get into more mischief.

One July afternoon, Kathy, Paula (my older cousin), Kim, and I heard a tap-tap-tapping in the grassy backyard. To our delight, Boy, wearing his wife-beater undershirt, hammered away, building an outdoor playhouse for the four of us. He collected eight old window screens from the garage and deftly constructed a magical play castle (with added mosquito protection). Once our mansion was finished, we moved right in. Dollies and doilies surrounded us, and we pilfered plastic dinnerware and coffee cups from the kitchen cupboards. Winded from his construction project, Grandpa plopped down in a lawn chair to observe the festivities. We served him lukewarm *Ovaltine* and *Vanilla Wafers*. The four of us climbed around our screened cage like a family of spider monkeys until suppertime.

My grandfather was a master chef. His calorie-laden country cuisine caused every dinner guest to pack on the pounds, but I loved every gorgeous bite. Every dish started the same way. Boy pulled out his cast iron skillet from beneath the stove, grabbed his coffee can full of bacon grease and fried up a storm. Meals were taste-less without bacon grease. We dined on fried chicken, chicken fried steak, fried catfish, and fried okra. Even turnip greens were filled with ham hock and bacon grease. Turnip greens made Boy's way were "larapin' good." If Boy wanted to get little sister Kathy's goat, he'd yell "turnip greens," and shove a spoon toward her lips. She shrieked in horror, ran lickety-split, and hid under the bed. Boy laughed so hard his sides hurt.

The *piece de resistance* of backyard picnics was homemade peach ice cream. It was the highlight of my childhood. This delicacy was not sherbet, sorbet, or ice milk; Boy's confection was the real deal.

To the canister chock-full of sun-ripened peaches, Grandpa added a quart of heavy cream and a pound of sugar. The ice-cream maker sat in an old aluminum barrel stuffed with newspaper. Boy methodically sprinkled ice and rock salt around the metal canister while we turned the crank. Thirty minutes later the "cream" had firmed up and the dasher was removed. I still salivate when I think of that scrumptious dasher full of peachy goo globs. Each child got a lick, and then the ice cream maker was iced and packed while we downed our dinner. All culinary experiences pale in comparison with "peach ice cream ecstasy"—the brain freeze resulting from rapid consumption of the confection. If Boy had been there when *Baskin and Robbins* were creating their thirty-one flavors, all thirty would have been superfluous. Peach was enough.

After we consumed our carbs and calories, our taut little bellies slowed us to a delightful stupor. We sat dazed in front of the boob tube, watching *Elmer Fudd* and *Pepe le Pew* cartoons until bedtime. A sleepover at our grandparents' house was the perfect ending to the perfect day. As the orange sun peeked through the pecan tree, Kathy, Kim, Paula, and I donned our pj's and climbed into Boy's four-poster bed. The fat, furry squirrels that leapt from limb to limb in the massive pecan tree that covered the backyard with shade and nuts mesmerized us.

Bedtime stories by Boy usually began with the resident fluffy-tailed super hero, *Johnny Squirrel*. Johnny stuffed his huge cheeks with pecan "bullets" and machine-gunned his enemies into submission. His prey fell to the ground, pelted and pecan-crusted. Johnny finally returned to his tree-trunk den and radio headquarters. Grandpa Boy didn't narrate his stories like any old grandpa. He was a ventriloquist. After having *Huey, Dewie and Louie* tattooed on his right foot, he wiggled his toes to make their tiny ink beaks talk. The ducks kept the story line going.

As the evening shadows beneath the pecan tree grew longer and darker, Boy's adventure tales became scarier. An ominous *Gee-Whizzicus* surreptitiously slinked over the back yard fence, ready to skewer unsuspecting Johnny and roast him for a bedtime snack. Johnny assumed his best Kung Fu pose and soundly defeated his monstrous opponents.

Wallygoppers were especially dangerous enemies because they could climb pecan trees and hang from the branches like the flying monkeys in *The Wizard of Oz*. The tussles between Johnny and Mr. Wallygopper were intense but short-lived, because our little eyelids were getting heavy. Johnny gave Wally a devastating karate chop, sending him to the grass below. Boy knew we needed a "happily ever after" ending, so Johnny and Wally made a peace treaty as they downed pecan pie with whipped cream.

Four little cousins snuggled and snored on Boy's fuzzy chest until daybreak. By the way, can you imagine what we had for breakfast? Pecan pancakes, of course!

> *"Love is patient and kind. Love is not jealous or boastful or proud 5 or rude. Love does not demand its own way. Love is not irritable, and it keeps no record of when it has been wronged. 6 It is never glad about injustice but rejoices whenever the truth wins out. 7 Love never gives up, never loses faith, is always hopeful, and endures through every circumstance."* (1 Corinthians 13:4-7 NLT)

Paul the apostle eloquently describes love in this famous passage. Circle the adjectives that describe what love is and what love is not.

Verse seven paints a picture of enduring love. Who in your life has demonstrated these qualities? Which ones bless your life the most? If you did not receive genuine love from your family in your growing up years, find someone you trust to mourn those hurts with you and to give you comfort.

Picture God, your Heavenly Father. How do you view Him? Instead of the word "love" in 1 Corinthians 13:4-7, insert the words, "God, you are (patient and kind, etc)." Thank God for His love and compassion, and ask Him to reveal Himself to you more fully today.

Car Wars

Yesterday I sat at the stoplight, minding my own business, re-setting my iPod, scratching a mosquito bite, answering my cell phone, and peeling off my sweat socks. Then I noticed a familiar scene in my rear-view mirror: Car Wars.

A haggard mom in her well-stuffed checkered capris mooned me at the intersection of First and Vine. Red-faced and precariously perched between the front and back seats, she was hollering at the top of her lungs. Two little buck-toothed boys smeared with Coppertone and dripping with pool water were beating each other senseless. The freckle-faced, tow-headed kid clobbered his little brother in the head with a model airplane. Older brother fired back with a knuckle sandwich, followed by a head butt and a half-nelson hold. Fortunately, there were no cars behind us, so I sat through another red light to enjoy the show. The curly-headed baby in the car seat next to Mom peacefully sucked her binkie, oblivious to World War III behind her.

Once "Moon Mom" had peeled the two brothers apart, I assumed that order had been restored. But the fun was just beginning. Big brother, energized by the heat of battle, lobbed a Hostess Ding-Dong at Mom's ponytail scrunchie. Enraged, Mom careened over the curb into the Wal-Mart parking lot, ripped open the back door and tanned the hide of brother number one. I wanted to stay and watch the Mama drama, but a rickety truck filled with lawn mowers and weed whackers pulled up behind me, the driver leaning on his horn.

This all-too-familiar scene jogged my memory, taking me back to sister skirmishes of years gone by. My little sister, Kathy, and I basically tolerated each other. We woke up every morning, fell out of bed, and stumbled toward the kitchen in a stupor. Our early morning tussle began with who got potty privileges first. I jerked Kathy's *Minnie Mouse* jammies' trap door away from the john and jumped on the porcelain throne ahead of her. Infuriated and consti- pated, she kicked me in the shins, pelted me with Ivory soap, and tattled to Mother. Feeling very smug and satisfied, I was lured to the kitchen by *Post Crispy Critters* and bananas. Kathy left the kitchen in a huff to take her potty turn.

Round One: Julie 1, Kathy 0.

Colorful, glistening little "critters" were heaped high in my bowl. I sighed and sniffed my favorite breakfast treat. I was shocked and disgusted after I shoved the first sugary spoonful down my gullet. I nearly choked to death. Kathy had poisoned my cereal with salt and pepper when Mom had her back turned. A knock-down drag-out fight ensued in the hall between the bathroom and kitchen. Mother peeled us apart and sent us to our room, cereal-less and steaming.

Round Two: Kathy 1, Julie 1.

Momma thought her time-out plan would discourage further infighting, but she was wrong. She sentenced us to hard labor—cleaning out our disheveled closet—an incredibly distasteful task. Dr. Scholl had not invented *Odor-Eaters*, so the smell was nause-ating. We pulled out the sweaty shoes in stony silence. Shoe battling soon commenced. We pummeled each other with Keds until we both smelled like foot fungus. Mom stormed through the door and threat-ened us with solitary confinement if we didn't finish the job. The worst part of closet duty was clearing the cob-webbed corners. Our mutual fear of creepy crawlers unified us as we swabbed the base-boards with dishtowels and *Pine Sol*. No spidies surfaced! Fisticuffs were avoided.

The next phase of closet-cleaning was old toy removal. Toy ownership was always a bone of contention. Who owned the *Malibu Barbie*? Even though she was headless and buck-naked, we both claimed her as our own. "I got her last Christmas!" "Liar! She was my birthday *Barbie*!" "Was not." "Was too!" "Who gave her to you?" Lathered into a frenzy by our war of words, Kathy and I pulled poor *Malibu Barbie* apart like a chicken wishbone. She was so mangled after that, neither of us wanted her. *Winnie the Pooh* was next. Pooh was Kathy's bear for sure. He had slept under her arm since she was a tiny tot, but he was suffering from years of neglect. The tubby furball had been stuffed behind moldy beach towels and leftover *Legos*. When Kathy spied his dusty, disfigured form, she sobbed uncontrollably. For once, I sympathized with her. *Pooh* reeked of mildew and chlorine, so he was no longer fit to be her bedtime buddy. We solemnly processed to the backyard, read words of consolation from our *Picture Bible*, and laid *Pooh* to rest beneath the mimosa tree. Mom was so touched by our reconciliation that she gave us our lunchtime beanie wienies early.

Alas, our peace treaty was short-lived. Turf wars are inevitable between countries and children. Mattresses and back seats were hotbeds of conflict for Kathy and me. We drew the "invisible line" down the middle of the bed. If either sister poked a hairy toe across the line of demarcation, hair-pulling, finger-biting, and jammie-ripping ensued.

Road trips were the worst. Dad got so tired of the "my side, her side" quarrel that he pulled out the masking tape, measured the width of the back seat, and clarified the boundaries. This feeble attempt at preserving the peace lasted about fifteen minutes. Our rickety *Rambler* sedan wasn't air-conditioned, and the radio was broken. The "Are we there yets?" started before we hit the city limits. On a muggy June day, we were baked and bored. Kathy and I had to entertain ourselves somehow. We started with an innocuous game of *Cracker Jack* basketball. Each player would alternate chucking a caramel popcorn piece into the open mouth of the opponent. If the candy corn hit the target, the pitcher got a point. After two turns, the *Cracker Jack* toss got ugly. The popcorn pelting turned aggressive and a full-out food fight was born. Dad screeched the *Rambler* to a halt, threatened us within an inch of our lives and re-stuffed us into the back seat.

In a last-ditch effort at tranquility, the family engaged in a rousing rendition of *The People on the Bus Go Up and Down* and *Ninety-nine Bottles of Beer on the Wall* until we were too hoarse to croak. Harassment seemed to be the only activity that held any allure for us. The name-calling started first: "Pig Face." "Blubber-Belly." "Snot Nose." "Son of a Snitch!"

Our names got meaner, and our faces got redder. Mom whipped around and warned us of impending doom. Dad tried to divert our attention once more by playing the license plate game, but we were more interested in pinching. We could poke and pester quietly without arousing suspicion. Silently, surreptitiously, we tortured each other until one of us yelped in pain. Dad pulled into the 7-11, poured enough *Benadryl* down our throats to drug a horse, and we snored all the way to Galveston Beach.

Sibling rivalry is universal. Cain and Abel certainly started us all on the wrong foot. But Kathy and I buried the hatchet years ago. We've learned to play nicely!

Be devoted to one another in brotherly love. Honor one another above yourselves. . . . Live in harmony with one another. Do not be proud, but be willing to associate with people of low position. Do not be conceited. Do not repay anyone evil for evil. If it is possible, as far as it depends on you, live at peace with everyone. (Romans 12:10; 16–18 NIV)

This passage paints a clear picture of "brotherly love." Condense the principles contained in these verses into one sentence.

List the verbs and adverbs used in these verses. Are the words *devotion* and *commitment* synonymous? How are they different?

What does humility look like in practice? How might practicing humility change the atmosphere of your home? Please explain.

Great Scotts: Neighborhood Fun

T he Scotts, our next-door neighbors, were more farm-loving than kilt-wearing and bag- piping. Though Larry did come from a long line of highlanders, he never used "bonnie" or "lassie." Instead, he drawled a happy "howdy" and "evenin'." Larry's favorite Scottish cuisine was *McDonald's*. Dixie, Larry's perky wife, hailed from Beeville, Texas — a town the size of *Walmart*. Dixie was a cracker-jack cook, but her food choices were unpredictable. I often weasled my way to a place at the dinner table so that I could witness the bedlam of a Scott evening meal. Dixie eschewed Scottish cuisine like haggis and blood sausage, in favor of Mexican food. Dixie's favorite vacation was her honeymoon with Larry in Tijuana, pre-kid and pre-housewife. For one brief shining moment in her life, all Dixie had to do was lounge on the beach and sip tequila shots. (She grew up in a liberal Lutheran family). "Theme night" dinners were a regular family ritual. Dixie placed her souvenir sombrero in the middle of the dining room table and served up nachos, burritos, tacos and churros — anything that ended in "o" and was deep-fried in a vat of *Crisco*. Diane, the only girl in a houseful of boys, refused to partake, claiming that Mexican food gave her zits. Portly Larry downed double portions of burritos to calm his nerves after wrestling with his feisty brood all day.

Steve Scott, the burly eldest brother, was a meanie with sixteen years of troublemaking under his belt. He knew how to surreptitiously toilet paper the front yards of his enemies. He "oreoed" the car windshield of Earl, the nerd from math class. The oreo-er opens the crème filled cookies and places them face-down on the car glass. *Oreo* crème hardens like concrete and binds to the glass windshield indefinitely. Steve also held the all-time record at Sunset High for the most creative excuses to ditch class. Nobody messed with Steve. Little brother Dougie wisely steered clear of his older, tougher sibling.

Diane, the fifteen-year-old Scott sister, spent most of her day primping in front of her bedroom mirror. At school, Diane was hot stuff. At home, she padded around the house in brush rollers, her face slathered in white *Noxema* goo. Diane was shapely, seductive and sneaky. Her dad should have locked her in the closet and thrown away the key. Hour after hour, she giggled and purred on the telephone with every boy in the tri-state area. Scads of jocks, geeks, wimps, slobs, and redneck cowboys lined up outside the Scott front door, hoping for an audience with the prom queen. Diane had no use for her little brothers, Dougie and Donnie, and they were thrilled.

Donnie, the youngest Scott tot, had an aversion to clothes. He complained they were "itchy" and streaked around the house *au naturale*. Occasionally, Dixie misplaced him, and discovered Donnie skinny-dipping in their outdoor wading pool. That is how I learned about the birds and the bees. Little Donny pestered his big brother, Dougie, incessantly. He attached himself to his older brother like a barnacle to a boat. Dougie and I tried to get Donnie out of our hair by tying him to a bedpost and shoving a handkerchief in his mouth. He escaped like Houdini. We finally got rid of him by teaching him to play hide-and-seek with my little sister, Kathy. Dougie and I blindfolded them both, spun them around, and left them stumbling in the dark for hours. Finally, Dougie and I had a few minutes to misbehave without interruption.

Mischief and mayhem resulted when I conspired with my favorite next-door neighbor. Dougie was my best buddy because he was convenient. As soon as the sun rose, I shuffled through the backyard in my bare feet, threw open the rickety gate between our houses, and burst through his door unannounced. Dougie blindly followed any evil plan I concocted. Such devotion was given to me because he suffered mercilessly at the hands of three bullying brothers and sisters. My intimidation techniques seemed tame by comparison.

Our most heinous crime was burgling goodies from Larry Scott's garden. We knew if our theft were discovered, we would be grounded for the rest of the summer. Suddenly, Dougie and I had second thoughts. The wrath of Larry Scott was legendary. Nervous and guilt-ridden, we flinched at the roar of the lawn mower down the street. What if the vegetable police got wind of our mischief? A car roared into the Scott garage. Busted. Fortunately, big brother Steve was returning home from his weekly meeting with his parole officer. Diane was leisurely sun-baking on a lawn chair, oblivious to our antics. Our tattling little brother and sister were taking swimming lessons at the neighborhood pool down the street. This was our big chance.

The Scott backyard was a verdant paradise compared to ours. My mother and father had brown thumbs. Our yard contained nettle-infested grass, a clothesline, and a mimosa tree that dumped green dandruff all over our front porch. I look with envy at the Scott's aluminum swimming pool, the tire swing, and plump, delicious veggies across the backyard fence.

Dougie's dad had a fertile patch of ground filled with delicious produce: sweet corn, okra, beets, sugar-snap peas, and cherry tomatoes. Larry Scott spent most of his evenings and weekends hoeing, fertilizing, weed-whacking and grooming his earthen mistress. I'm not sure he ever saw his wife, Dixie. With her four hellions running willy-nilly through the house, poor Dixie was probably incarcerated in the sweltering garage by her naughty progeny.

The Scotts' beautiful vegetable garden was off-limits to errant children and hungry rabbits. We weren't sure, but Dougie's father warned of land mines in the row between the fence and the sweet corn. One particularly sultry July morning, Dougie and I could stand it no longer. We *had* to partake of the forbidden fruit (I mean vegetables.) Mr. Scott was at the hardware store, buying a weed-eater. He was so enamored with all things agricultural, we figured we had at least an hour to sneak a snack before he returned.

Now came the big decision — what would our booty be? Sweet corn was pretty tasteless without a pound of butter and some salt and pepper. Okra was too hairy. Nobody ate carrots, except the brave bunnies that lived behind the carport. Then we saw them — plump, ripe, red and round — bushes and bushes of cherry tomatoes. They shone in the sunlight like rubies. We though the word "cherry" meant they were filled with fruity goodness. I made Dougie fetch a bucket and a saltshaker. We surveyed the perimeter, scurried toward the tomato row, and plucked the delectable orbs as fast as our grubby little hands could pluck. After we had denuded three or four plants, we surreptitiously crept behind the shed to enjoy our forbidden fruit (I mean vegetables).

I expected to taste the sweet nectar of cherry pie filling when I bit into the first little tomato. To my surprise, armies of green seeds shot forth from the veggie like a bee-bee gun. All that was left after the initial squirt was a rubbery skin and some vinegary liquid. But our prize was too hard-won to waste. So we salted each little red bullet and shoved them in our mouths. It was almost lunchtime, so I downed twenty or thirty of them in ten minutes. Dougie, not to be outdone by a wimpy girl, did the same. We polished off the entire bucket just in time to hear our mothers' whistles summoning us for lunch. We hastily returned the muddy bucket and hurried to our respective houses, just in time for the midday meal. To my chagrin, my lunch plate was piled high with a cheese sandwich and oodles of little cherry tomato halves. One look at those seedy little red balls made the room spin and my seedy stolen snack returned from whence it came. Needless to say, the kitchen linoleum looked like someone spewed rotten salsa everywhere. I truly learned the meaning of the verse, "You can be sure that your sins will find you out."

Dougie and I were grounded for good. Dixie said I was a bad influence on her innocent little cherub, but I knew better. We devised our tomato robbery together. If Mr. Scott had not grown his garden so close to my chain-link fence, I never would have been tempted to steal. Or would I? I have since readily consumed summer squash, okra, corn, peas, and asparagus, but I never want to see another cherry tomato again.

The Scott family forgave our petty theft after a while, and continued to be dear friends. Mom and Dad sat in the porch swing with Larry and Dixie, chatting and surveying their yardfull of children. My heart warms when I remember my happy summer days with the kids next door. The amiable Texas brood made my childhood exciting and fun.

"Love must be sincere. Hate what is evil; cling to what is good. 10 Be devoted to one another in brotherly love. Honor one another above yourselves. 11 Never be lacking in zeal, but keep your spiritual fervor, serving the Lord. 12 Be joyful in hope, patient in affliction, faithful in prayer. 13 Share with God's people who are in need. Practice hospitality." (Romans 12:9-13 NIV)

This passage provides us with very practical ways to demonstrate Christ's love to others. Underline the verbs in these verses and describe what practicing them would look like in your own life.

What are some ways that you can love and bless your neighbors? How can you reach out to them? Do you know them well? Gone are the days when neighbors chatted across the fence. Do you make an effort to greet those who live and work near you?

Who has been a good neighbor to you? What kindnesses have they shown you? How did they bring joy to your life? Write down a special memory you have of a loving neighbor.

Nosey: Looking For Manure!!!

Noses are nifty little facial appendages. They sniff, smell, sneeze, snort and snore. Our noses are supposed to help us savor the scent of a flower or to take a whiff of my Aunt Ivelle's *Summer Rose* toilet water. They were designed to warn of danger and help us taste our food. But mostly, noses run, bleed, and provide an endless supply of crusty nuggets for mischievous little boys to pick and flick. Noses come in all shapes and sizes: pug, pointy, perky, flat, flared, hooked, and stubby. One might think that human schnozzes would surpass the olfactory skills of God's lowly creatures. Nothing could be further from the truth. My golden retriever, Surely, can sniff the hiney of a Doberman and immediately know if he is a fast friend or fiendish foe. My vet, Dr. Poage, tells me that a canine can sniff a puppy pal's poop and determine the sex, age and kind of kibble his doggie buddy scarfed. Boy doggies sniff chair and table legs to see if interlopers have invaded their territory and peed in their domain. Goody, my pesky, overly suspicious Corgi, leaves a yellow trail around my grand piano legs to show who's boss of the house.

"Nosey" is an adjective that describes someone who sticks his nose where it doesn't belong: in someone else's business. "Curiosity killed the cat" is a warning for people and puppies alike. Some stones should be left unturned. Snuffles, the paunchy tabby down the street, became bald as a billiard ball when he "curiously" sniffed and pawed the *Sunbeam* hair dryer precariously perched on the bathtub ledge. Snuffles was never the same again. His litter box was moved to the garage.

Marge Mooshew, the hefty alto in the church choir, was overly "curious" about every member of Cockrell Hill Baptist Church. Marge lingered in the bathroom stall to hear the latest tasty morsel about Art Palmer's late hours at the office. She was convinced Jody Boyd, the church secretary, swiped ten-dollar bills from the Sunday offering plate. How else could she pay for that fire-engine red patent leather purse? Pastor Jones must be a ladies' man, Marge surmised, because he slathered way too much *Brill Cream* through his brown, wavy locks. Behind every coat closet and water fountain, Marge gleefully gleaned her gossipy tidbits. Armed to the teeth with half-truths and innuendo, she began her calling crusade. Marge phoned Peggy, Peggy dialed Betty, and Betty called the entire Women's Missionary Union to warn them of chinks in the pastor's armor and skeletons in the deacons' closet. With each phone call, the fibs were fabricated and the sins of the saints grew. By the time Ethel Bentley got the scoop, Art Palmer was a pimp and Pastor Jones was an axe murderer.

Marge's nefarious nose must be stopped up! Pastor Jones preached a fiery four-sermon series on "The Tongue is a Fire" from the book of James, but Marge remained clueless, even when her husband Ed elbowed her in the ribs. She "amen'd" and cried, "preach it, Pastor," glaring at the sinners and backsliders seated in the row behind her. Marge really needed a nose job. Someone should have lobbed that sucker clean off her face. Nothing seemed to faze the self-appointed "Baptist private eye." She was sure the finger pointing applied to someone else.

Nosey Marge began her career as a snoop at a very early age. Her sniffing skills fueled fires among her playmates when she was in elementary school. Little Marge had a knack for scrawling the latest tasty bits about her Sunday School classmates on the toilet stall wall. "Vicky Palmer is a stooge." "Sara Sulley cheated on her boyfriend Harold." "Elma Studder fudged the answers on her math test." The lies went on and on and on. The problem with Marge was that she was cool. Nobody wanted to question her inside information. She got a smug satisfaction from wrecking people's lives. Her training as a rumor mill landed her a cushy job in college as a gossip columnist for the *Mabank Post*. A self-proclaimed "private eye," meddling Marge lurked in the back of Fred's coffee shop and skulked around the boys' locker room door. The delicious secrets Marge stole were published for the entire world to see.

As Marge grew older, she was oblivious to her shortcomings. She always couched her remarks in the form of "prayer requests." "Pray for Velma Peabody," she moaned. "God has revealed to me that she has fallen off the wagon and hit the bottle again." "Didn't you see the rum raisin cake she brought to Wednesday night dinner?" Big deal. Paul told Timothy to take a little wine for his stomach. It was first-century Pepto-Bismol. "Pray for Stuart Depew," she whispered, "he's got a thing for his Sunday School teacher." What thing? Doesn't every middle school boy chase a skirt or two? Hormones are hormones. Give the kid a break.

But the Good Book warns, "...you can be sure your sin will find you out." Marge stuck her snoopy schnozz out too far. Elba McElroy wandered over to our little congregation from the Methodist church down the street. Not enough sewing circles... When Elba joined the Baptist biddies, Marge had met her match. Elba gave her a taste of her own medicine. If Marge had "roast preacher" for Sunday lunch, Elba had "roast Marge" for Sunday dinner.

Elba invited Marge and Pastor Jones to her house for pie and coffee, and Marge had to face Pastor Jones, eyeball to eyeball.

The Holy Spirit did the rest. The moment Marge returned to her old tricks and started the phone chain on the latest scandal, Elba grilled her for the details and checked her story. Marge finally decided the manure she was shoveling wasn't worth the trouble. She had been cut down to size and the snooping stopped. If I had given monikers to the seven dwarfs (not small in size, but small in soul)

I might have named them Grumpy, Grouchy, Lazy, Fussy, Sleazy, Nasty and, the worst, Nosey.

Now the only thing Marge Mooshew sniffs is warm chocolate cookies straight from the oven. We should do the same.

King Solomon had much to say about the sin of gossip. Perhaps he saw the destructive nature of slander in his bevy of 700 wives and 300 concubines. I'm sure there was no love lost between his bevy of beautiful women. Here are just a few observations from the wise king:

> *"A gossip betrays a confidence, but a trustworthy man keeps a secret."* (Proverbs 11:13 NIV)

> *"A perverse man stirs up dissension, and a gossip separates close friends.* (Proverbs 16:28 NIV)

> *"A gossip betrays a confidence; so avoid a man who talks too much."* (Proverbs 20:9 NIV)

> *"Without wood a fire goes out; without gossip a quarrel dies down."* (Proverbs 26:20)

How does Solomon describe the character of a gossip? How do gossip and slander damage relationships? What are some steps you can take to avoid gossiping about others? Circle the key-words in the above passages.

Picture Jesus listening to your conversations. Is He smiling? Does He see a pure heart and a genuine love for others in you?

Spend some time praying about your words, and ask God to help you believe the best about your words concerning others, and ask God to give you a grace-filled tongue.

Creepy Crawlers

Bugs give me the willies. They always have. They always will. If I had my way, I'd strap a ten-pound can of Raid to my back and wear a pair of size thirteen stomping shoes for spider-smushing. My jungle-dwelling missionary friend, Kristina, told me that she was happily drying her post-shower behind when a tarantula the size of her head appeared on the dry side of her towel. Though she grew up in a conservative Baptist home, she learned to dance a mean jitter bug in her skivvies that morning. If I had stood in her shoes (or bare feet, as the case may be), I'd be dead from heart failure. I haven't even mentioned the baby boa constrictor she found in her son's closet!

You may deny bug aversion, but everyone is scared of something. Just Google a list of phobias. *Ablutophobia* means fear of bathing. Men were born with that one. *Arithmophobia* is a fear of numbers. I've had that one since algebra. *Alektraphobia* is the fear of chickens. Colonel Sanders had that one, God rest his soul. Fears abound under every letter of the alphabet. You can have *xyrophobia*, fear of razors (my husband has that one, too), or *zemmiphobia*, fear of the great mole rat. Bats (the flying kind — not the wooden kind) give me the willies. Mice, snakes and aggressive geese cause me to shake and shiver. Losing my car in the mall parking lot is a perpetual fear, probably because I do it at least once a week. However, every other fear of mine pales in comparison to my bug loathing.

There are no creepy crawlers in heaven. How do I know? Insects are of the Devil. Remember the Egyptian plagues and the locusts of Revelation? I rest my case. "Thus saith the Lord, 'Neither bug-geth, nor wormeth, nor roacheth nor spidereth shall inhabit my holy home.'" 1 Julie 1:24. I believe Paul the apostle penned a verse or two about dogs being in heaven and cats being in hell (although I'm not quite sure). I'm praying Effie, my ferret, out of purgatory. She was a biter.

Four-eyed entomologists swear that we need insects to bal-ance the earth's ecological system. They teach that *Kermit the Frog* and the *Geico* gecko would skip supper without a few fried flies and pickled potato bugs. Don't worry about the amphibians. Let them check out the dollar menu at *Taco Bell*. If it's good enough for Chihuahuas, it's good enough for froggies. In my estimation, a bugless world is Utopia. In a perfect world, fire ants couldn't zap my ankles and torment my pudgy dachshund, Beauford. In a perfect world, cockroaches couldn't infest my sugar bowl when I go on vacation. Mosquitoes couldn't feast on my flab when I hike through the woods, and ticks couldn't torment my golden retriever when she forages through the oleanders. In Utopia, centipedes can't find refuge behind my guest room toilet on a hot June day, and desert scorpions wouldn't wag their stinger tails on my patio in devilish defiance.

Invisible pest predators are the worst. During my preschool summer days, chiggers infested the lush bermuda grass in my back-yard and took up residence between my toes. The more I scratched, the more they itched and scooted around underneath the skin on my lumpy feet. Daddy said nail polish would suffocate the little boogers, but Mom disagreed and washed me in a chigger soap that smelled like rotten eggs and black tar. The chiggers died, but nobody would sit next to me at Vacation Bible School. Tiny black ants surreptitiously invaded my chocolate chip cookies at the church picnic and added extra zing to my red *Kool Aid*. The wicked stings of "no-see-'ums" at the lake (Daddy didn't know their proper ento-mological classification) gave me welts on my posterior. Yes, the most irritating bugs were the ones I couldn't see!

My abhorrence of all things "insectual" began at an early age. Elvis Tiggle lived two doors down and hoarded mayonnaise jars filled with nasty creepy critters. A wolf spider (not werewolf), a cricket (not Jiminy), a praying mantis (really an agnostic), a katydid (oh, no she didn't), and a beetle (not the band) rounded off Elvis' collection. Elvis' mother bought him a set of pipe-cleaner antennae at the five-and-dime. He skulked around the neighborhood garages, lurking in dark corners, just waiting to pounce on unsuspecting little girls like me. I retaliated with a spray bottle of Windex. The goopy cleaner wasn't poisonous, but it made his little antennae wilt and stick together. Elvis' bug-bullying reached new heights when he was allowed to bring his monstrous arachnids to show and tell in second grade. Petula the tarantula appeared on top of my boiled carrots more than once. I swore off vegetables until Thanksgiving. Thank God, Petula ignored my *Three Musketeers*!

My second grade teacher, Mrs. Snyder, assigned us partners to create an insect collection for science class. Much to my chagrin, weasly Elvis Tiggle was my partner. Why, God, why? Couldn't I have some dainty little girl who liked grasshoppers and butterflies? But God was on my side all along. I let Elvis grab all the bugs he liked. He gassed 'em and speared 'em. All I had to do was draw little nametags on *Post-it It Notes* with *Magic Marker* and purchase cheap frames at the drug store. It was such an easy "A" that I picked Elvis again when it was time for frog-dissecting. I smiled behind my mask and stood a safe distance away while Elvis gleefully chopped up all the froggy guts. Our frog didn't survive his "frogectomy," but Elvis and I passed amphibian surgery with flying colors.

Ladybugs and doodle bugs were safe "little girl" insects. If you gently touch a doodle bug on his roly-poly black back, he'll scrunch up into a little ball and roll down the sidewalk. Doodle bug marbles and doodle bug bowling were favorite summer pastimes for my sister and me. However, my sister Kathy preferred ladybugs. Their bright red and black spotted shells made them fashion icons of the bug world. Florescent butterfly wings flapping in the breeze paled in comparison, fireflies glistening in the night sky were a "flash in the pan," but ladybugs were practically perfect in every way. Lulu, our favorite ladybug, minded her manners when she scuttled up Kathy's forearm, tickling only a little bit. She didn't even holler when my little sister pulled off a leg or two.

I hold the firm belief that most women marry for the sole purpose of having someone large and brave around to do all of the cricket chasing and spider smashing. Men can also prove useful for light bulb screwing and pan scraping. Other than that, males are totally superfluous to our existence. (Well, almost!) The splat of a June bug flattened on my car is poetic justice for the horrendous emotional trauma I have suffered from creepy crawlers through the years. I feel a sense of wicked exhilaration knowing that my windshield is the last thing going through his little June bug mind.

When I see something hairy or squiggly, I simply call my husband's name and my hairy "shoe fairy" rescues me from peril. He is my strong, brave Terminator. I shall fear no weevil.

Satanic attacks are often unexpected and invisible. They surreptitiously suck the fun out of life. Demon-bites of the enemy can get "under our skin" and cause us misery and fear. *Baal* in the Bible means "lord of the flies," and the baals of Israel were the bane of their existence. We must put our own idols aside and find our rest and protection under the shelter of a powerful God who loves us, and a Savior who has trampled Satan under His feet.

"Those who live in the shelter of the Most High will find rest in the shadow of the Almighty. 2 This I declare of the LORD: He alone is my refuge, my place of safety; he is my God, and I am trusting him. 3 For he will rescue you from every trap and protect you from the fatal plague. 4 He will shield you with his wings. He will shelter you with his feathers. His faithful promises are your armor and protection. 5 Do not be afraid of the terrors of the night, nor fear the dangers of the day, 6 nor dread the plague that stalks in darkness, nor the disaster that strikes at midday. 7 Though a thousand fall at your side, though ten thousand are dying around you, these evils will not touch you. 8 But you will see it with your eyes; you will see how the wicked are punished. 9 If you make the LORD your refuge, if you make the Most High your shelter, 10 no evil will conquer you; no plague will come near your dwelling. 11 For He orders his angels to protect you wherever you go. 12 They will hold you with their hands to keep you from striking your foot on a stone. 13 You will trample down lions and poisonous snakes; you will crush fierce lions and serpents under your feet! 14 The LORD says, "I will rescue those who love me. I will protect those

who trust in my name. 15 When they call on me, I will answer; I will be with them in trouble. I will rescue them and honor them. 16 I will satisfy them with a long life and give them my salvation." (Psalm 91:1-16 NLT)

Recall some occasions when you have experienced the protection of God. From what did He protect you? How do these verses address the fears you face?

List some of the word pictures that are used in this psalm to describe perilous situations. Have you found yourself in the same predicaments as the psalmist? How did you feel when you were going through them?

What are God's promises of deliverance and protection? List them here. Make a card of these promises and place them in your car and in your home.

The Bad Seed
Secret Scandal!

I come from a long line of crazies. Let me shake my family tree for you. I found some flavorful fruit, a few lemons, and one really rotten apple. In a society of people searching for significance, we long to know who we are and why we are here.

The East Texas morning sun streamed through the windowpane of the neighborhood *McDonald's* as I scarfed my *Egg McMuffin* and slurped my decaf *McCoffee* (two sugars). My Mom and Dad described the "fruit" that fell from my family tree in days gone by. They told of dirt farmers, gas jockeys, oil barons, rodeo cowboys, engineers and, oh yes, one bad seed. Every family has one. It's the renegade relative who makes Aunt Prissy and Uncle Baptist blush. The black sheep. I'm sure every family closet has its share of skeletons, but the bag of bones from our "Tacker Tree" takes the cake.

We were always a colorful bunch. I discovered today that my great-granny Evelina seldom wore underwear. It cramped her style.

A farm wife and all-around tough cookie, Evelina skinned squirrels and wrung chicken necks before you could blink an eye. Blood
and guts never phased her. She only saw the squirrel stew and fried
chicken that would fill her table after the dirty work was done. My
father, Ralph Jr., told me of the redneck wife of our rodeo wrangler
who swilled beers and swore like a sailor. First Cousin Shirley was
a sharp shooter. She could pick off a squirrel in mid-air with her
twenty-two and shoot an unsuspecting bunny before the squirrel hit
the ground. Nobody, but nobody, messed with Cousin Shirley.

One shady character from the Tacker tree stood out from the
crowd. He was the name you mentioned in hushed tones — the page
that was missing from the family Bible. Daddy's fifth cousin (twice
removed), Elderberry Waldo, was the talk of Thanksgiving dinners
and Saturday night bridge games. Daddy told me that he possessed
a treasured scrapbook of Tacker lore, but Elderberry was conspicu-
ously missing. How could he speak of this cousin with such shock
and awe? My daddy was no saint. When it came to mischief, Dad
came in a close second. At three, he experimented with a nail and
an electric socket and nearly blacked out the neighborhood. I think
his preschool foray into electrocution caused him to lose his hair at
an early age. At nine, Ralphie jumped off the garage roof, assured
that he could fly like *Superman*. He survived unscathed, except for a
well-deserved whipping. At eleven, he carved a foot-long scar in his
sister's leg with a coat hanger, and at eighteen, he was arrested by
the campus police for engaging in a rousing bout of fisticuffs.

Elderberry, however, took the cake. My dad's earliest memory of his errant cousin involved a slingshot and a wasp nest. Apparently wasp larvae were used as fishing bait, so Elderberry clipped the nest, full of wasps and all, and sent it hurdling to the ground. This was not a smart move. One particularly enraged wasp returned the "shot" with a sting between Elderberry's eyes. Elderberry swelled up like a bowling ball. He couldn't even see the nest, much less fish with the wasp eggs. Ralph's cousin was either extremely brave or extremely stupid. As history would have it, he was both.

Elderberry soon morphed from mischievous to malicious. He tired of writing spelling words and being sent to the principal's office for classroom crimes, so he burned down the Malone school. Now that's what I call over-reacting! Once he tasted the adrenaline rush of being the town bad boy, there was no stopping him. My father rolled his eyes as he recounted the tale of Elderberry's car chase with the Texas Highway Department. The evil cousin's drab *DeSoto* couldn't go above 40 mph, so he lit a dynamite stick and hurled it in the window of the pursuing cop car. From misdemeanor to mastermind, Elderberry's robberies and scams finally succeeded in placing him upon the *U.S. Most Wanted* list along with Al Capone and John Dillinger. One drizzly Saturday afternoon, a patrolman pulled Daddy over for speeding. (Of course, he was only five mph over the speed limit!) When the cop saw Pop's last name and mug shot on his driver's license, he shook in his boots. Sheriff So-and-So, the brawny Texas lawman, thought he was face to face with the legendary Elderberry Tacker. Dad is not sure if Elderberry was placed behind bars for his many crimes, but he sure led a colorful life. Our family was tainted. Though we had our share of saints and sweethearts, we all knew about the cagey con man that tarnished the family name.

My father wondered if he could have rescued his childhood playmate from his wicked ways. He pondered long and hard about his cousin's criminal bent and wished he could have seen the signs to save Elderberry from himself. Daddy's last memory of his errant cousin was a telltale one. Elderberry shivered on his front porch and asked to borrow Ralph's father's overcoat. Texas winter winds were biting to the bone, and Ralph Sr. worked outside pumping gas in the bitter cold. During those war years, nobody owned more than one coat, so my dad was sure Elderberry would return it right away. Elderberry smiled, winked, and sauntered down the lane. He was never to be seen or heard from again.

We all know an Elderberry or two. However, we also have a little of Elderberry in all of us, to one degree or another.

My maternal grandmother, Dora Goodman Tacker (affectionately called "Moy") wasn't a bad seed, but she had a few weedy qualities. My Grandma was a ring-tailed tooter. She built airplanes in World War II, she pumped gas in the forties, and she was a smooth-talking real estate saleswoman until she was ninety. Yep, those Tacker women were tough as nails. Though we adored her moxy, Grandma Tacker lacked tact. Whatever she was thinking promptly popped out of her piehole, unedited and uncensored. Her wit was razor-sharp and her criticism was on the catty side. Such frankness proved effective when she collected the monthly rent from her tenants. And she collected the dinero herself until she was ninety-two! If you crossed Moy, there was hell to pay. Though my grandma was short in stature, she held onto a grudge like a bulldog with a bone. Years later, she'd pull out your scorecard and remind you of your many mistakes.

That "steel trap" mind of Moy's also remembered every birthday, every graduation and anniversary. She partied hearty and loved passionately. Dora knew our faults, but often gave us grace. Her tenacity translated into fierce loyalty. She loved God, her family, and her Sunday School ladies. Moy taught the Bible with heavenly wisdom until her dying day. But she drove to church like she was headed for Hades.

Most of us are not miscreant ne'er-do-wells like Elderberry. We are a mixed bag of sweet and sour like Moy. Whether you see yourself as Elderberry or Dora, or someone in between, you can be different today. Jesus died for you, warts and all. When you accept God's free gift of salvation, paid for by Jesus' painful death on the cross, you are born again with heavenly DNA. God trades your sinful seed for the seed of Christ. You are born again. He turns your tares to wheat, and gives you a new family and a Heavenly Home.

As we encounter the Elderberrys in our lives, may we look with deep compassion upon them, realizing that without a Savior, we would walk in their shoes. We must never fail to share the promise of unconditional love, forgiveness and transformation that Jesus offers.

> *"Therefore, if anyone is in Christ, he is a new creation; the old has gone, the new has come! All this is from God, who reconciled us to himself through Christ and gave us the ministry of reconciliation: that God was reconciling the world to himself in Christ, not counting men's sins against them."* (2 Corinthians 5:17-19 NIV)

Do you remember what your life was like before you met Jesus? What are those things that make you vulnerable to sinning against God? What triggers you to run from the God who loves you so much?

What does "reconciliation" mean? Look it up in the dictionary. Is a "reconciler" a mediator? Or does it mean more than that? The passage states that God did not count our sins against us when Christ paid the price for our misdeeds. How does that make you feel? List some things in your life that make you feel guilty. Picture Jesus, reaching out to you with complete forgiveness and acceptance. Meditate on His forgiveness today.

Spend some time thanking God for your new life in Him. Ask God to bring to your mind those near ones who need a touch from you. Who can you encourage today? With whom can you share the transforming message of the gospel?

When Granny Comes Marching Home...Again!!!
The Relatives Are Coming!

This particular Christmas morning had a frosty nip in the air and clear-flying skies for Santa. Kathy and I had ripped the paper off every present by 6:00 a.m., fought tooth and nail over every Barbie and wiffle ball, and had eaten half of the *Candyland* pieces. (Nobody told us they were plastic...) To our bleary-eyed parents' chagrin, we finished Christmas "cheering" before breakfast. By noon, the troops started rolling in: extended family members from Fort Worth, Fairfield, and Post Oak. *Ford Fairlanes* and *Chevy* pickups rattled up the driveway, bringing our country kin. Those were the days when *Fords* were *Fords* and *Mitsubishi* was the sushi place down the block. A glitzy *Cadillac* glided to the curb, carrying our upscale cousins and their pharmacist father. My maternal grand-parents took up two city blocks with their boat-sized *Impala* (that I later inherited for college). Grandpa Boy and my grandmother Moy

Tacker (named by my eldest cousin before she could actually gurgle a name) pulled up in a shiny red *T-Bird*. They sold real estate up into their 80s and drove flashy cars to dazzle the clientele. I would definitely buy a house from someone spunky enough to schmooze and peddle houses when most folks their age were hitting the nursing home.

Every vehicle was loaded to the gills with gifts, coats, covered dishes, and decorations. Kinfolk poured out of their cars like clowns tumbling from a *Volkswagen*, racing toward our front door. Dad and Mom were breathless from stashing away wrapping paper and wrestling us out of our fuzzy footy pajamas decked with holly. All children should be entitled to pad around the house in sleepwear until noon on Christmas. But no, my sissy and I had to be gussied up for the family feast — barrettes, bows, brushed teeth, red and green jingle socks, and shiny patent leather shoes. By Christmas dessert, the hair bows drooped, the gravy was dripped, turkey strings hung from our molars, and our shoes disappeared beneath the tablecloth.

The tribal ritual continued. Grandma Moy burst through the door first. You could hear her belly laugh from three blocks away. She sashayed into the living room like she owned the place, toting a bejeweled purse the size of Alaska. Moy handed off her homemade chocolate pie to Mom and planted a plum-passion lipstick kiss on each of her adoring grandchildren. Moy dressed flamboyantly, just like her car, with crystal earrings, a sequined sweater, and crimson high heels. She reeked of White Shoulders perfume. We adored her.

When we went to Moy's house on weekends, she let us try on all her flowered hats and jewelry bling. We created sexy satiny dresses out of her lacy petticoats and stumbled around in her stilettos. Although Moy was lively and fun-loving, she had the annoying habit of giving us a plethora of white cotton panties every Christmas. What could be more revolting? Toys were prominently displayed in every shop window, but Moy traipsed right past them to the underwear department. Finally, when we became teenagers, Moy branched out and bought us panty hose.

Ma Blakely, affectionately known as "Ma B," was my Mom's mom. Ma B always smelled like cornbread. She lived on a small East Texas farm most of her life, and her meals were hearty, homemade, and full of homegrown ingredients like pickled okra and canned pears. In the kitchen, Ma B was a genius with a cast-iron skillet. She was also a remarkable seamstress. Even though Ma B was poor as a church mouse, her gifts were works of art. Kathy and I always received delicately embroidered dresses with matching dolly clothes that she had sewn, knitted, or crocheted.

Grandpa Blakely, "Pa B," smelled like *Old Spice* and peppermints. He was very dapper in his striped suit and tie, replete with silver cuff links. Pa B had moved up in the world from dirt farmer to grocery store manager. He was a self-made man and proud of it. Pa B often cashed in a few bills at the *Safeway* and brought us handfuls of quarters and silver dollars. Eventually, we had a shoe box full of them, and we used them to purchase our college textbooks.

Bad investment! If we had foresight, we should have held onto those silver dollars. They would be worth a fortune now. What a waste!

Grandpa Boy was hands-down my favorite relative, even to this day. Amid the array of cousins and chaos, Boy always had time for me. I climbed into his lap anytime, day or night, and he always had a hug, a *Hershey's* kiss and a yarn to tell. Boy often got down on all fours with us, and whinnied and pawed as we played horsey. We were usually full of fudge and cookies by then, so he truly became a beast of burden. By the way, Grandpa Boy never gave me underwear. When I was three, he bought me a toy piano. When I was four, he gave me a xylophone, and when I was six, he bought me a real piano I still play to this day.

Once the "grand" entrances were made, the hoopla started. The men folk lumbered in like bulls in a china closet, knocking unsuspecting Christmas balls off the tree and converging upon the television set before the kickoff. Joke-telling, back-slapping and Frito-munching filled the living room. Once the men were ensconced in their bubba chairs and ottomans, they didn't seem to mind us kids playing tag around the living room (during half-time, of course). Bedlam erupted as all the cousins tore through the house. Aunt Ivelle and Grandma Moy guffawed with giggles so loud they broke the sound barrier. The women remained in the kitchen. To this day, I am unsure why Christmas day was a segregated event. The ladies always chatted, cooked, and cleaned the kitchen wreckage while the men lazily lounged in their comfy pants (worn especially when serious eating was to be done).

Christmas feasts were potluck dinners at our house. Everyone brought a covered dish, for better or worse. Boy, sweet Grandpa that he was, toted his oyster stuffing to the feast. Oysters should be banned by the Food and Drug Administration. Any food that slides down your throat without being chewed is both disgusting and dangerous. To mix such hideous shellfish with cornbread is a travesty! Pretty Aunt Ivelle always brought mincemeat pie – a lame excuse for dessert. After all, if a dessert had "pie" in the title, it was supposed to be tasty. Whoever had the bright idea to mix meat and fruit had to be an idiot! My first cousin, Paula, told me some Count in England invented mincemeat, and I believe he should have kept it to himself along with goose liver, spotted dick, and figgy pudding.

No one ever knew which fowl to serve for Christmas: turkey (been there, done that at Thanksgiving), goose (who knows how to cook it?), and game hen (way too measly for the guys). Out of desperation and total lack of consensus, we always sold out for ham, sweet potatoes, and green-bean bundles. As a kid, the rule-of-thumb was to move the meat and vegetables around the plate so it looked like you ate them, and then tank up on the chocolate pie and sugar cookies.

Occasionally, our get-togethers would include Pastor Jones and his family. I was excited because I had a crush on Buddy, the eldest Jones boy. He didn't know I was alive. All he cared about was who would get the gizzard (or ham hock, depending on the holiday). Normally, Pastor Jones blessed everything and everybody. Before church services, weddings, dinners, or funerals, Neal Jones intoned eloquent words to the Almighty. But this Christmas would be different. Daddy sanctimoniously gathered the troops from the sofa and backyard. We all held hands and bowed our heads for the blessing. He said, "Julie, it's your turn to pray." This was my big debut. At long last, I was chosen to say the pre-feast prayer. I closed my eyes and began to thank God that I could still hold my sister at arm's length when she tried to punch me in the stomach. I praised God that Mom always left one warm chocolate chip cookie on the cookie sheet for me to munch. On rare occasions, she let me grab a ball of raw cookie dough without her reproach. I glorified God that my buckteeth wouldn't be shackled with rubber-banded braces until I was eleven. I was pleased that the ushers didn't mind if I chomped my chewing gum during church, and I was especially blessed that Ma B allowed me to dump as many marshmallows as I wanted into the sweet potato casserole.

Just as I started to get rolling, Daddy elbowed me and quietly suggested that I pray for more important things. (After all, Pastor Jones was listening.) So I puffed out my chest, took a deep breath and pontificated in hallowed tones.

"Dear LOOOORRRRDDDD, I thank Thee for Thy beauteous bounty and Thy sanctification." Sanctification was a big word I often heard in church, and I assumed it had something to do with

Santa's vacation. He would definitely need one after Christmas was over. I pleaded with God for the welfare of the children in Africa, beseeched him for every sick person I knew, and even interceded for the President of the United States (even if he were a Democrat.) Dad cleared his throat to urge me to wind it up, but I was on a roll. Finally, when the meat was iced over and the biscuits were burnt, I said "Amen." For some reason, no one ever asked me to bless the food again.

After dishes were done and ball games were won, the Christmas bash was over. The hugging ritual commenced once again and promises were made to get together more often. The truth is, you can't improve on perfection. We all knew that holiday family reunions came but once a year and should be savored like a gourmet meal. At sunset, the Grannies went marching home…again!!!

Psalm 127, one of the psalms of ascents the Jews sang on their way to Jerusalem, celebrates family. Enjoy the poem, and let it remind you of holiday gatherings gone by.

> "*3 Children are a heritage from the LORD, offspring a reward from him.*
> *4 Like arrows in the hands of a warrior are children born in one's youth.*
> *5 Blessed is the man whose quiver is full of them.*
> *They will not be put to shame when they contend with their opponents in court."* (Psalm 127:3-5) NIV

Think about your family. Some may be loveable, some may be challenging to love. Take some time to thank God for His gift of family.

How does the psalmist describe children in verses four and five? Why are they like "arrows"?

Are you building a family legacy? Think of ways you could make special memories with your relatives. What are some relationship-building activities you could share? What are some traditions you would like to create? What kind of memories will you want your children or grandchildren to have?

That's Showbiz!

My stunning showbiz career began at age five. One crisp September morning, I stormed the stage with a convincing depiction of a broccoli stalk. The play was *Tummy Ticklers*, and each class member was heroic or villainous according to FDA approval ratings. Only the skinny girls could play carrots and corn. Since I had a portly posterior, my permed green hair added symmetry to my somewhat pudgy stalk. The roughage got to cut a rug because we were nutritious, so the carrots, corn, squash and broccoli leapt around the stage, captivating crowds before *Veggie Tales* was ever invented.

Hamburgers, cheese fries, and donuts lay motionless on a heap of yellow beanbag fat cells. The audience was instructed to cheer for the veggies and boo for the junk food. This moralistic tale of nutrition gone awry didn't have much impact on us as kindergartners. As soon as we finished the show, we high-tailed it to the lunchroom to down our *Oscar Mayer Wieners*, *Cheez-its*, and *Twinkies*. I paid a high price for my veggie debut, however. I tried to wash the green *Jell-O* out of my hair for a week, but the green powder simply faded my dishwater blond locks to the color of snot.

The Christmas pageant at church was my next gig as a serious actress. I was decked out to the max. I donned my red velvet dress, lacy socks, and black patent Mary Janes. Mommy scrubbed my face 'til it was raw and brushed my teeth well for the first time since I polished off my Halloween candy.

Our family arrived at church shortly before the sun went down. Miraculously, Mom had kept me out of mud and mischief for a full hour. I stood in the cherub choir assembly line with thirty other wiggling, squiggling five-year-olds. The choir room at church looked more like hell than heaven. Little demons tussled and scuffled with each other—pulling hair, whining, and kicking each other in the shins.

Undaunted, "Use your inside voice," Mrs. Francie hollered, to no avail. Meanwhile, the mother-helpers gingerly grabbed the bratty kids first and shoved square white tablecloths over their heads. The trick was to wedge the little singers between the chair and the table while pinning the bows on at the collar. Red bows, some vertical, some horizontal, and some resembling Boy Scout knots were hastily attached to each caroler. Before we went onstage, Mrs. Francie cleverly bribed us. She promised that any child who sang without hair-pulling, hand-waving, or booger-picking would be rewarded with a block of Christmas fudge following the concert. Such a yummy prize definitely motivated us to behave, but some of the moms wondered if they really wanted to take their little charges home hopped up on sugar and caffeine.

Finally, all conceded that the show must go on. We lumbered onstage holding each other at the waist like a mini-conga line. Then, upon the director's cue, we made a sharp right face and looked the congregation members square in the eye. Mrs. Dudley, the organist, eagerly awaited her cue to charge through the intro to *Joy to the World*. Most organists love this hymn because it only uses one organ foot pedal. It's tough to mess it up. After we belted four verses and a chorus of *O Come, All Ye Faithful*, we exited the stage to prepare for the Nativity scene. Having squirmy five-year-olds make a costume change was a big blunder. The intermission took longer than the program as frantic mommies searched for the right bathrobe for each child.

Casting for the manger scene was challenging. Mrs. Francie picked Eddie and Dickey to be shepherds because neither could carry a tune in a bucket. Reggie, Todd, and Buddy, the three kings, came from the first-grade class. Our patient choir director observed that they exuded self-importance and dignity. The kindergartners knew the truth. The only reason they seemed self-assured was because they beat the living daylights out of unsuspecting four-year-olds on the playground. That didn't seem like "wise" behavior to me!

Randy Phelps was a shoo-in for Joseph, because he was the tallest kid in the class. Unfortunately, Randy also had a short attention span, so he spent more time horsing around with Eddie the donkey than paying fatherly attention to Mary and baby Jesus. Ellen Stuffle claimed the Mary part because she still had all of her baby teeth. Always the *prima donna*, Ellen monopolized the toilet, constantly glopping on grown-up blush and lip-gloss, and demanded a fresh towel headdress at every rehearsal.

Once again, my stocky shape made me a natural pick for livestock. Manger mammals were selected according to size: boys were camels and donkeys; girls were sheep and goats. Eddie, the class clown, was thrilled with his donkey role. He "hee-hawed" his way through the program in his most convincing *Eeyore* voice. My "baas" were better than my "bleats," so I played a barnyard sheep. I didn't realize at the time that this was the worst possible role to play. Our furry sheep costumes were hot and itchy. After three sweaty rehearsals, my wet hair was plastered to my head, and I reeked like a cow patty.

Tilly Tingle clawed her way to the top to assume the starring role of Christmas angel. Angel auditions were cutthroat, so Tilly brown-nosed the teacher by clapping erasers in Sunday School and bribing her with Christmas saltwater taffy. All of her efforts paid off. In the end, Tilly floated atop her cotton-ball cloud and warbled *Silent Night*. Stars like Ellen and Tilly had their own paparazzi. I remained content to "baa" in the background and blend into the sea of angel wannabes. Thus concluded my career as an extra waiting in the wings.

The Tacker girls loved anything musical or theatrical. Although I was content to be a sheep or vegetable, my sister, Kathy was destined for stardom. She was a full-blown scene-stealer. At three, Kathy demanded a captive audience, forcing extended family members to offer undivided attention and applause while she clogged endlessly on the bathroom tile with Mom's stilettos. If parents and grandparents weren't around to watch her warble and hoof, Kathy pulled nearby neighbor kids away from *Mickey Mouse* to play her adoring fans. Nicknamed "Tiger Lil" by my father, Sissy roped me into working full-time as her manager and wardrobe designer.

Before breakfast every morning, Kathy plopped on my peacefully slumbering body and demanded that I style her curly blonde locks into a *Cinderella* bun as soon as we downed our *Eggos.* I painstakingly pinned her ponytail into a yellow lump and sprayed it with *Aqua Net* until it remained stiff and motionless the rest of the day. Bows and barrettes were added according to her fancy. After hair and makeup were complete, we combed the closet to pull out the old lace bedroom sheers Grandma Moy willed to us when they were too shabby to remain on her windows. We used rubber bands, safety pins, and an oversized rhinestone brooch to create magical wedding dresses and ball gowns.

Kathy was determined to be a headliner on the *Ed Sullivan Show* along with Mr. Ed and Ringo. Mom and I rolled the grocery cart around *K-Mart,* and Kathy practiced her act by standing up in the shopping cart seat, throwing her arms out, and crooning *Blue Suede*

Shoes in front of the *Frosted Flakes*. If other shoppers failed to pay attention, she'd just modulate to a higher key and use a black-eyed pea can as a microphone. By the time we hit the cash register, she was signing autographs. Once Kathy could finally stuff her little rotund shape into a sequined leotard, she was unstoppable. She tap-danced, tiptoed, cartwheeled, and belly-danced for anyone who looked her way.

Tiger Lil's first taste of stardom came when she nabbed the famous "mirror ball" trophy at the John W. Carpenter talent show. She warbled a compelling rendition of *Big Bad Bill is Sweet William Now*. (I'm quite serious—that was the name of the song!) I believe she had absolutely no idea what those lusty lyrics meant, but the grownups sniggered and awarded her first place for her gumption. Most of the time I accompanied Kathy on the piano, but our dynamic duet her second-grade year was a showstopper. We pulled on fishnet tights, furry tails, and kitten ears. We shimmied and shook our way through Bobby Rydell's number-one pop hit *Alley Cat*.

> *He goes on the prowl each night, like an alley cat.*
> *Looking for some new delight, like an alley cat.*
> *He meets you-meow, and loves you-meow, and leaves you-meow . . .*
> *Like a Catsanova does.*

Where did we find such seedy lyrics? Apparently, grade-school censorship was at an all-time low. In spite of our song choice, the crowds went wild. We still perform encores upon request.

Kathy and I held onto the center-stage spotlight as long as we could. We performed a litany of recitals, concerts and musicals, and begat offspring every bit as splashy and uninhibited as ourselves. Our sequins, gowns, and feather headdresses are tucked away in plastic bubble wrap and cotton balls. But every now and then when we're feeling low, out come the tutus, tiaras, and tap shoes.

> *If you have any encouragement from being united with Christ, if any comfort from his love, if any fellowship with the Spirit, if any tenderness and compassion, then make my joy complete by being like-minded, having the same love, being one in spirit and purpose. Do nothing out of selfish ambition or vain conceit, but in humility consider others better than yourselves. Each of you should look not only to your own interests, but also to the interests of others.* (Philippians 2:1–4 NIV)

According to Paul in his letter to the Philippians, what should our motivations be for treating others with humility and love?

What do we receive from God in order to meet the needs of others?

Verses three and four describe our human tendencies to be proud and self-centered instead of humble and others-centered. Do you struggle in these areas? Please explain.

Imagine what it would be like to put this passage into practice. What would it look like in your life?

Practice rejoicing over victories and mourning over hurts with the people God brings into your life this week.

Dog-Paddling And Water-Walking Troubles With Bubbles

Jesus walked on water. The apostle Peter did too (for the most part). My sister and I needed a little help in the water-walking department. One balmy June morning in my sixth year of life, Daddy tried to teach me the fine art of "cannon-balling" off the diving board into his awaiting arms. He failed to notice my little sister, Kathy. Lil was aggravated at being ignored and decided to swim to the deep end where we were splashing. To three-year-old Kathy, her idea of swimming was a brisk walk on the bottom of the pool. Dad shot toward her like a rocket and carefully explained that there is no air under the water. Mom was a landlubber. She thought it unladylike and distasteful to get wet in public. After a heated discussion, they concurred that we needed swimming lessons.

Our parents enlisted Mavis Wilford to "water-proof" their little girls. Mavis Wilford (we nick-named her Mavis Wafflebottom) had leathery, pruny legs the size of tree trunks. Her faded, checkered swimsuit with the pleated petal skirt had seen many summers of dog paddling and breast-stroking. (That didn't come out right!) Mavis was hard-core. Nobody left her class without a respectable *American crawl.* I'm sure Mavis was Baptist, because her first lesson included a swift kick to the rear and full immersion. Her little charges bobbed to the top, screaming and sputtering. But their little arms flapped and their fat feet kicked 'til they stayed topside. Gentler swim teachers wasted time with gentle bubble blowing and face dipping in the shallow end. Wimps.

I helped my little sister, Kathy overcome her fear of drowning by giving her daily swirlies. The "swirler" took the victim's head, plunged it in the toilet bowl, and flushed repeatedly. If the "swirlee" didn't learn to hold his or her breath underwater, Mavis' water-Nazi dunking would be terrifying. I was just trying to prepare Kathy for Mavis. Really. My water-boarding techniques worked. Kathy was the star of the class, puttering around the pool perimeter like Nemo the fish.

One summer, my Mom got creative and sent us to the YWCA swim camp. Because of Mavis, we were "pros" at the butterfly and sidestroke. The teacher was impressed and subsequently enrolled us in synchronized swimming. Synchronized swimming is bad ballet that is invisible to the naked eye. Most of the graceful underwater moves could only be spotted from a Goodyear blimp flying high over the turquoise pool water. Everyone else had to guess the choreography from the poolside metal bleachers. Our teacher showed us how to pirouette, leap, twist, and turn for hours. At least we avoided summer mosquitoes and chiggers. Our favorite move was the "rotating pyramid." Kathy hopped on my shoulders and threw out her best jazz hands as I spun beneath the water like a blender. Our career was short-lived. Kathy couldn't seem to hold her position on my shoulders without emitting little gas bubbles from her behind. Enough is enough. Our "tower" toppled and we ended up trading punches by the ladder in the deep end. Mother was heartbroken. She had spent her Saturday mornings as a child watching Esther Williams — some 1940s starlet. Esther ended every movie diving sideways into a pool with sixty other scantily clad swimmers. Together they formed intricate underwater flowers. I'm not sure Esther could act, but she sure could fill out a swimsuit. Mom had high hopes that we would swim our way to stardom. Fat chance.

Once we were "swim-certified," Mom drove us to the Red Bird public pool for an afternoon of swim-fin fun. She dropped us off at the pool entrance and retrieved us two hours later when we were pooped and sun-drenched. We paid our twenty-five-cent admission fee and strolled toward the wire swim cubbies to lock up our belongings. I can't imagine anyone bringing "valuables" to a public pool. All we brought were towels and thongs. Thongs were not sexy underwear. They were fifty-cent flip-flops purchased by moms to protect kids' toes from "pool shower foot fungus." The wire cubbies had mini-padlocks and keys to secure your stuff. My question is, where is a girl to stash her key? How many little-girl swimsuits were equipped with pockets? We spent half our time at the pool trolling the bottom for our little key, and usually found twenty others next to ours.

I was unaware of the perils of public pool sanitation. Why didn't little boys leave the pool to pee? Kathy and I would potty every thirty minutes or so because we swallowed so much pool water. When I discovered much later in life that boys liked to pee in the pool, I was horrified! And what about those un-potty-trained babies bouncing with Mommy in the shallow end? Did they wear diapers? Did they not? EEEWWWW! Creepy crawlers — automatic pool vacuums — had not been invented. The only cleanup between pool use was a tired teenager who skimmed the water for June bugs, nose plugs, and "already-been chewed" gum.

By the time Kathy and I reached third and sixth grades (respectively), our pool time was occupied with gawking at the hunky lifeguard. Hank Ottoman (not the stool, not the empire) presided over Red Bird pool, slathered in Coppertone sunscreen and sporting snazzy sunshades. We adored Hank. He had the physique of a Greek god. Even his muscles had muscles. Hank Ottoman blew his whistle periodically just so Mr. Arnold, the pool owner, actually thought he was paying attention to the little peons below. My sis and I spent most of our mornings getting glamorous for Hank. After hours of mani-pedi- cures, we peeled on our fluorescent Speedos and flowered rubber swim caps. We practiced holding our stomachs in until we suffocated. Kathy and I were certain Hank would fall off his perch, dazzled by our beauty. Our flat chests, horn-rimmed glasses, pimples, and braces somehow escaped Hank's notice. Hank only had eyes for luscious Lucy Pettijohn. Lucy was well endowed for her fourteen years and painted her mom's red lipstick on her bee-stung lips. Lucy had practiced running on the concrete in slow motion by watching back-to-back episodes of *Baywatch*. Her hard work paid off. Hank was mesmerized. We think he took a long lunch break to practice mouth-to-mouth resuscitation with Lucy.

Our only hope of capturing Hank's attention was to pretend to be drowning. Drowning is serious business. Cartoons always showed drowning victims holding up fingers "one-two-three" to alert others of their last gasping breath. Nobody noticed our finger distress signals because we were standing in three feet of water. Only once did we see Hank spring into action. Swifty, our freckle-faced neighbor, paddled into the deep end and was clipped by a diver off the high board. Hank shot off his perch like a rocket and valiantly saved little Swifty. After that, we decided distracting Hank was a bad idea.

Pool afternoons were positively perfect with the exception of "pool bullies." They dunked you beneath the chlorinated waves until you choked and sputtered for air. Pool bullies were worse than school bullies. During the school year, these creeps only had thirty minutes to taunt us on the playground. Summer afforded them much more time to perfect the art of intimidation. Their aggression was fueled as they studied the nefarious *Wiley Coyote* constantly harassing *Beep-Beep the Roadrunner*. Cartoon violence gave them much more ammo to torment us. Our only recourse was to tattle to Mr. Arnold. The pool bullies were sentenced to beach towel time for fifteen minutes. That didn't seem like much punishment for the indignity we suffered.

Swimming, no matter how leisurely or strenuous, made me famished. Kathy and I topped off our afternoon fun with a *Nehi* grape soda and a *Moon pie*. *Moon pies* were s'mores without the campfire. The afternoon snack was so delicious, we didn't care if our tummies pooched. We were water-tired, baked, and bronzed. What a way to spend a day!

To this day, we are grateful to Mavis for the aquatic skills we learned from her. Strong and sturdy Mavis was not affable or patient, but she got the job done. We could dive, thrive, and shoot across the pool confidently and consistently.

The laws of hydrology never change. Water-displacement and buoyancy will support any human, no matter how portly or clumsy. Jesus' power and character never alters. He will always be there. He will never, ever let you drown. Displace your doubt with faith. Stop floundering and start floating. Start faith-ing and stop fighting. Your spiritual journey will allow you to graduate from bubble blowing to dog paddling to lap swimming to diving in the deep end. The more you trust, the more you know Jesus, you will be "walking on water" before you know it!

"Then he (Jesus) got into the boat and his disciples followed him. Suddenly a furious storm came up on the lake, so that the waves swept over the boat. But Jesus was sleeping. The disciples went and woke him, saying, "Lord, save us! We're going to drown!" He replied, "You of little faith, why are you so afraid?" Then he got up and rebuked the winds and the waves, and it was completely calm. The men were amazed and asked, "What kind of man is this? Even the winds and the waves obey him!" (Matthew 8:23-27 NIV)

The storm was raging around the disciples and they called for Jesus in their distress. Have you ever felt that your life was spinning out of control? Why? Did you call on Jesus to still the storm?

What do you learn about faith from Peter's water-walking experience? Peter began to drown when he took his eyes off of his Savior and onto the storm. Are there times when your faith begins to waver? List them here.

What do you learn about Jesus from verse 27? Meditate on the infinite greatness of the universe. Can you imagine Creator-God controlling all of it? Imagine the "storm" you are facing right now. With your eyes of faith, see Jesus stilling the storm for you.

Notice the story following this passage in verse 28. What do you learn about Christ's supremacy over the forces of nature?

Pray for God to give you His peace today.

VBS Story
Jesus And The Flannelgraph

Vacation Bible School was my favorite event of the summer. Just about the time the chiggers started biting and the crickets started chirping, the dear little old ladies in our church saved elbow macaroni and scavenged for *Popsicle* sticks in the neighborhood trash cans.

After muggy June days filled with boring TV re-runs of *Captain Kangaroo* and *Howdy Doody*, all my neighborhood buddies joined me to line up outside the church porch pillars. The whistle blew promptly at nine o'clock and we marched through the doors to a rousing version of *Onward Christian Soldiers*. It was positively euphoric! The pianist, usually the child who had completed Book Two of *John Thompson's Piano Course*, limped through two or three stanzas of the hymn and then plinked the famous "sit-down" chord so that we would ceremoniously take our seats on the rickety wooden pews. I thought Mozart was credited with the "sit-down" chord progression, but the Baptist Sunday School Board claimed it originated with the Baptist Hymnal composers. Besides, Mozart was not around to defend himself.

If you didn't throw spit-wads during the Bible story or pull your neighbor's pigtails, Lonnie, the middle-school helper, might pick you to be flag-bearer for the morning's pageantry. The taller boys got to hold the American and Christian flags so they wouldn't drag the ground during the pledge. I call that sexual discrimination. I could wave that spangled banner as well as any sixth grade boy. But the girls were relegated to hold the Bible for the Bible pledge. The slackers had to pass the offering plates. We faithfully brought our pennies and nickels to help the missionaries in exotic countries we couldn't even pronounce. I still wondered if the twenty-five bucks we raised would make a dent in Ethiopia, but I believed God saw our offerings and smiled.

You couldn't wear shorts to VBS in my day. Shorts were of the Devil. I didn't like them anyway, because I had hairy knees. However, I always thought the dress code was a paradox because dresses were so hard to keep from floating up on the see-saw. The real reason I attended VBS was for the red Kool-Aid and graham crackers. You'd think they had pulled out hot fudge sundaes and whipped cream. But our Bible school workers believed in asceticism. If graham crackers were good enough for Jesus, they were good enough for us.

The mommies who "didn't have a real job" were conscripted into the "army of the Lord" for VBS week. Their daunting task was to convert all the little hellions into saints by Friday. To my mind, some of the mean little boys in my class could not possibly be "convertible." Every mommy had spent painstaking hours after their kids were asleep cutting felt, sorting beads, and scavenging for pine cones. I still swell with pride when I remember the exact replica of King Solomon's temple I made with toothpicks, pipe cleaners, and tongue depressors. The one controlled substance in our class was glitter. For us, it was the star dust from heaven we tossed in the air to make everything sparkle. Glitter was only permitted on Friday, because it took two days for Stanley the janitor to sweep it up.

My favorite VBS sport was the re-enactment of Moses parting the Red Sea. Billy Bob Turner got to play Moses. He was given a long white cotton beard and a choir robe. Billy Bob, looking very spiritual, pointed his "rod of God" broomstick and used his best *Charlton Heston* voice to command the water to part. As mini-Israelites, we took our turns on the slip-and-slide, pretending to cross the sea to dry land. I can't imagine the Jews had as much fun as we did. We weren't worried about the Egyptians; we just loved to body-surf between Israel and Egypt.

Noah's Ark Wednesday was the high point of the week. Every child lugged a pet from home and we shoved our furry buddies in the cardboard boat (a refrigerator box with a sheet for a sail). Of course, we always had an odd number of creatures, so the animals entered the ark one-by-one instead of two-by-two. Monty's python had a field day. He ingested two white mice and a gerbil before the ark landed on "dry ground."

When Mrs. Tuttle, our VBS teacher, ran out of ideas, she told the story of Ruth. Ruth was the Moabite hottie who harvested grain in Boaz's field. Boaz liked what he saw and immediately popped the question. The rich farmer threw down his sandal at the gate of the city, and requested the city fathers would permit him to claim Ruth as his bride. This Bible story led to pandemonium. Tuttle threw un-popped popcorn on the floor and told us to "glean" while she sipped her Nescafe. "Gleaning" occupied us for several minutes. Then the sandal-throwing started and we pelted each other until recess.

Each summer, we had a "token man" besides the pastor to be the heavy for Bible school. Usually this poor guy was Harvey Pettle, a retired deacon too tired to say no to his wife. Our lone father figure in a sea of estrogen enforced discipline when an incorrigible bully tried to wreak havoc during the devotional. If Stuart Depew or any of his cronies were too hard for Harvey to handle, they were banished to purgatory – the pastor's study – until they repented.

Bible drills were a big part of Christian combat training at VBS. We clasped our Bibles tightly, threw out our chests like boot camp recruits, and waited for the Bible battle cry. "Attention," the teacher bellowed. "Draw swords." Our "weapons" were poised straight ahead like AK47s. "James 5:6. James 5:6. Charge." We flew through the pages like greased lightning. Arnold, the snooty kid with the red-letter edition, always got there first. He might not be able to read all the words, but he found it, by golly! I still sing the "Books of the Bible" song when I can't find Obadiah.

Our church playground was not as fancy as the school's, but we loved it just the same. The jungle gym was as familiar as an old shoe. It resembled the leaning tower of Pisa because Mr. Grigsby had soldered its creaky joints so many times. We only had six swings, a merry-go-round and a couple of seesaws, but surprisingly, everyone took turns. You just couldn't be too annoying with Jesus watching.

My favorite part of every morning was the flannelgraph story told by Mrs. Brumit. *Veggie Tales* videos would come decades later, so cardboard Jesus would have to do for the time being. Our teacher had carefully trimmed each Bible character and glued felt backing to every disciple. The chalkboard was covered with a felt baby blanket so each figure would stay put. Miraculously, Zacchaeus stayed up in the sycamore tree with nary a thumbtack or Elmer's glue.

Though Jesus' puny silhouette drooped more as the week passed, He grew bigger in my heart just the same. I felt His warm presence, and I knew my life would be different. Jesus was real and He always talked to me at VBS. I stopped beating up on my little sister and prayed my goodnight prayers more fervently.

Yes, Vacation Bible School was the pinnacle of my summer vacation. My mom so enjoyed the break that she shipped me off to the Methodist Bible School the following week. But the Methodists

were much more liberal. They let us eat devil's food cake and no
one cared.

> " *¹ How lovely is your dwelling place,*
>   *LORD Almighty!*
> *² My soul yearns, even faints,*
>   *for the courts of the LORD;*
>   *my heart and my flesh cry out*
>   *for the living God.*
> *³ Even the sparrow has found a home,*
>   *and the swallow a nest for herself,*
>   *where she may have her young—*
>   *a place near your altar,*
>   *LORD Almighty, my King and my God.*
> *⁴ Blessed are those who dwell in your house;*
>   *they are ever praising you."* (Psalm 84:1-6 NIV)

Write down some of your memories in experiencing God's presence. Do you feel the longing that the psalmist felt to come into His presence in prayer and praise? What did He say in those quiet moments? How did it make you feel?

Does church seem like "God's House" to you? Are you glad to go to church? What are some ways that being a part of a church body enriches your life and your family?

Spend some time in prayer, thanking God for His manifest presence when you worship Him. Pray these verses from Psalm 84 aloud and personalize them. Make them your own.

Daddy and His Little Secretary Secretaries Galore!

The secretarial pool at my father's office was a menagerie of ladies. Each species bore unique markings, trademark behaviors, and occupied special habitats. Grizzly Gertrude Brown lumbered through the office front door promptly at 7:59 a.m. The shuffle of her orthopedic wedgies on the checkerboard linoleum struck terror in the heart of every copy boy and mail room clerk. When Gertrude entered a room, everyone saluted and instinctively knew that they must be guilty of something. Gertrude always wore her beige cable-knit sweater (did she ever wash it?) and polyester pants. Her salt and pepper bun was pinned so tightly to her head that it pulled her eyebrows up and made her look perpetually surprised. Two or three sticky notes clung precariously to the back of her pants legs when she ambled toward the file cabinet. In spite of her idiosyncrasies, Gertrude had the office purring like a well-oiled machine when she was on duty. Gertrude had joined the firm shortly before the crust of the earth had cooled. Nobody, but nobody, messed with the Grizzly.

Lee Gaddy, the willowy flamingo receptionist, was purely window dressing. Her strappy pumps were six inches high and she typed a whopping twelve words a minute. All of the execs peered out of the window when Lee pulled into the parking lot to spy her latest flashy, feathery ensemble. Lee was flirty, but, unfortunately, she was two fries short of a *Happy Meal*. On a good day, she could actually remember the name of the company and take down a coherent message. Like the sleek pink flamingo, Lee preened and strutted her stuff until quitting time.

Mary Sue Moore was the office hound dog. She sniffed out the office ne'er-do-wells and tattled to their supervisors. Mary Sue surreptitiously tiptoed into the break room in hopes of hearing the latest juicy gossip tidbit or discovering the newest intra-office romance. Once she got the scoop, Mary Sue wiggled her tail, shook her jowls, and howled away. Secrets weren't safe and snooping was an art form when the hound dog came to work. Most of the time, Mary Sue gave people the benefit of the slop, but in her defense, employees were motivated to keep their noses clean and their dealings above board.

Paula Froman, the hyena, was positively a people person. She cackled at the latest joke and told tales around the water cooler. Paula remembered everyone's birthday and put out the punch, pound cake, and piñatas to celebrate. No one was actually sure what Paula did at the company, but when she punched in, the party started. Her hyena high jinks were legendary. Mischievous office pranks like toilet-papering Brian's convertible or *Saran-Wrapping* the ladies' toilet seats were her forte. I loved Paula because she could make necklaces out of paper clips and earrings out of foil chewing gum wrappers.

Shy Patsy McCormick, the ostrich, seldom emerged from her cubicle. Patsy was the 'bean-counter' assistant accountant for the firm. She found socializing with office personnel as appealing as Chinese water torture. Small talk eluded her, so she arrived before anyone else and stayed late until everyone left the building. Patsy's desk was immaculate — perfectly appointed with pencils sharpened, papers color-coded, and files carefully alphabetized. She never made a mistake. She carried her 'ones' and crossed every 't.' Every office needs an ostrich to stay afloat. Occasionally Patsy let me into her 'hole in the sand,' and when she did, I felt special.

My mom, the golden retriever, was the company controller. Mom made sure that Daddy's imagination didn't exceed his assets. Mom hung in there with Dad through thick and thin. Every day, Mom retrieved my sister Kathy and me from school after a grueling day at the office and greeted us with a cheerful smile. Every morning, my retriever Mommy faithfully cut the crusts off our tuna sandwiches, sliced up half a pear, and stuffed two *Pecan Sandies* in our lunch boxes before she left for the 'war zone' at work. On Saturdays, she joined us in playing catch-up with the laundry and sink scrubbing. In sickness and health, for better or worse, Mommy stayed the course.

Gertrude, Lee, Mary Sue, Paula, Patsy, and Mommy made my dad's office a fun place for a little girl to visit. I often burst through the front door and made a bee-line for Lee's candy dish. She always let me take the green M & M's and leave the brown ones. Gertrude stopped barking orders long enough to hand me a red Marks-a-Lot and a pad of lined paper to keep me quiet and out of trouble. Patsy let me play with her spare calculator. I carefully typed in the numbers, turned the crank, and waited for the rat-a-tat-tat to spit out the answer. Calculators weren't digital in my day. They were happy number crunchers that made me feel like a math whiz.

Most days, I would sneak into the architect's office while Mom met with Gertrude or Patsy. The drafting tables were enormous — and high swivel chairs were just waiting to spin me into orbit like a rocket. I think my imagination was aided by sniffing the strong fumes of developing fluid that filled the room. Brian, the architect, showed me how to use a t-square and compass. I got to scribble on the giant vellum paper used for drawing plans. Bryan told me to keep my masterpiece a secret because drafting paper was expensive. So I finished my work of art, jumped out of his lap, and scampered to my mom's office.

Dizzy and delighted, I stumbled into Mom's inner sanctum, aglow with joy from all my office adventures. Being the boss's kid had a few perks. Nobody complained about my visits interfering with their workday. Years later, I spent many summer afternoons filing and typing at Dad's office, but I have always cherished the early days of *M & M's* and t-squares.

My happiest memory of entering my father's business world was the sunny March day Dad chose me to accompany him on a business trip to Ohio. He said he needed 'his best secretary,' and I filled the bill! Although I was only nine, I knew I could be his 'go-to girl.' Mommy packed my red polka dot dress, my ruffled petticoat and my no-nonsense oxfords. Daddy wore his best pinstripe suit and confidently strode into Armco's boardroom with me in tow. I pushed out my chest and gave everyone in the room a firm handshake. I even had my own nametag. Daddy introduced me as his executive assistant and the board members grinned and chuckled.

I whipped out my spiral notebook to take dictation as the meeting commenced. I scribbled as fast as I could, but words like *joint-venture* and *sub-contractor* did not appear on my second-grade spelling word list. If I didn't know what to write, I drew a picture of big buildings and hoped Daddy would be inspired. Finally, I lost interest and pulled out my *Lady and the Tramp* coloring book. For the first time in my young life, I sat quietly at the mahogany conference table without squirming or asking to pee.

Daddy was so proud. He picked me up and gave me a big bear hug as we left the meeting. To celebrate, we had chili dogs and chocolate ice cream — the food of the gods. Our business trip concluded with a hair-raising taxi ride to the airport. The yellow cab driver let me turn on the meter, and when we boarded the plane, the flight attendant showed me the cockpit and gave me a set of plastic wings. Could life get any better than this?

I snored in Daddy's lap the entire way home, dreaming of hot dogs and skyscrapers. As I awoke, Daddy told me what a good job I did. I was sure my presence at the meeting cinched the deal. The day I spent as Daddy's little secretary was a marker day in my life. He blessed me with his approval, his affection, and his respect. I felt so special, and I couldn't imagine anything better than hanging with my Pop.

That trip with my father reminded me of the blessing God the Father pronounced over His Son, Jesus. Christ was just beginning His ministry. He had not performed a single miracle. He had not preached a single sermon. But as Jesus stood with John the Baptist in the murky water of the Jordan River, His Father's voice rang in His ears. "This is my Beloved Son, in whom I am well pleased."

"Jesus came from Galilee to the Jordan to be baptized by John. 14 But John tried to deter him, saying, "I need to be baptized by you, and do you come to me?" 15 Jesus replied, "Let it be so now; it is proper for us to do this to fulfill all righteousness." Then John consented. 16 As soon as Jesus was baptized, he went up out of the water. At that moment heaven was opened, and he saw the Spirit of God descending like a dove and lighting on

him. 17 And a voice from heaven said, "This is my Son,
whom I love; with him I am well pleased." (Matthew
3:13-17 NIV)

**Meditate on the words God spoke over His Son. How do you
think this blessing made Jesus feel? Did someone in your life
ever impart *the blessing* to you? How did they make you feel
valued and accepted? What did they say or do that impacted
your life?**

**Put yourself in Jesus' shoes. John was right. He was unworthy to
baptize the Son of God. But Jesus responded with an enigmatic
answer. "Let it be so now; it is proper for us to do this to fulfill
all righteousness." What was the "righteousness" that needed
to be fulfilled? Was it God's plan to create this opportunity to
affirm His Son? Was it God's way of launching Jesus into public
ministry? Was it to assure Jesus of His divine heritage? What
were some other reasons God might have had to allow His Son
to be baptized by John?**

**Can you think of some people in your sphere of influence who
need your "blessing" and encouragement today? Who are they?
What will you say?**

Bullies

Bullies . . . those nose-picking, skin-pinching, shin-kicking meanies could be lurking anywhere. Over-sized ne'er-do-wells ambushed me from knotty, shaded oak trees on the playground. They stormed my back yard when I least expected it and pilfered cream-filled *Hostess cupcakes* from my Barbie lunch box. In all fairness, these rock-'em, sock-'em bad boys felt justified in terrorizing their female victims because they held the firm belief that all little girls had cooties.

Pudgy, *Brillo*-headed boys scared the beejeebees out of me by ambushing me behind the slide and tickling my armpits while I was happily swinging on the jungle gym. I bit the dust every time. Recess was particularly perilous. The bullies were hard at work. Leathery tetherballs socked me in the face and pounded my braces into my cheek. Soccer balls flew at my unsuspecting girlfriends from every direction, and I won't even mention the unspeakable acts committed during Thursday morning dodge ball matches in the sweat-infested gymnasium.

When Davy (let's call him "Butthead") Lewis pilfered my pink snowballs in the lunchroom, he stuck out his marshmallow-and-coconut-covered tongue and taunted me mercilessly. All I had left was a soggy tuna fish sandwich and some stale *Cheetos*. Lunch became a battlefield where skittish girls huddled together to hold onto their junk-food booty.

Apparently, bullying behavior in males can emerge as early as two or three years old. My second cousin, Gary Willard, began his career of intimidation at the ripe old age of four. He was an early bloomer in mischief. We were playing Cowboys and Indians. Gary claimed the heroic role of the Lone Ranger, and Donnie Scott, our next-door neighbor, donned our feather duster to play Tonto—the brave Indian sidekick. As for Silver, I got the job. For the next two hours, I winced in pain, hobbling around the living room on all fours while Gary, perched on my back, kicked me in the ribs and hollered "Hi-O Silver, away!"

After suffering a sore back and a severe case of rug burn, Silver revolted. I bolted out the front door, grabbing Gary's white cowboy hat, and trampled it in the sticky mud surrounding our red bud tree. A girl can take only so much horse humiliation, and I had reached my limit. Thus began my hatred of all bullies, great and small.

Dickey Dickert made first grade miserable for most of my gal-pals. Aside from having dandruff and bad breath that would curl your toes, Dickey was creative with his pesky pranks. He salted my lime Jell-O when I went to buy my milk, or he gave me a wedgie as I sauntered to the front of the class for my book report. For Dickey, spit wads were child's play. He lobbed play dough grenades covered in snot and saliva and carefully placed wads of wet Double Bubble gum on the linoleum under my desk. Mrs. Chase, our teacher, heard my screams, but Dickey was conveniently preoccupied puzzling over a math problem, looking angelic and innocent.

I remember the day my second grade world ceased to be Utopia. I thought as long as I was kind and courteous to these cranky fellows, bullies would be nice to me. That Utopian dream crashed down around my little ears when I was eight. Buddy Bell, my second grade nemesis, hated me to the core. Looking back, Buddy probably saw me as a snot-nosed, smart-mouthed teacher's pet. However, in my juvenile brain, I was the soul of grace and charity. Buddy was the hall monitor. Chubby Buddy wrote "traffic tickets" to speedy students who ran in the hallways between classes. Now that I look back, why would anyone *run* to class? Pop quizzes and math problems awaited us. But when Tubby Bell was around, I crept, I strolled, and I loitered. I did anything except run. Yet I still received the dreaded ticket that entitled me to a leisurely afternoon of detention hall. Why would he treat me this way? I spoke peace to Buddy Bell, but he declared war.

Fourth grade terrible twins, Buzz and Jimmy McKinney, struck fear into the hearts of every little girl in L.O. Donald Elementary

School. Buzz and Jimmy turned terror into an art form. They were the worst kind of villains—after-school bullies. Day after day when the bell rang, Lana Rouse and I donned our back packs to hightail it toward home. As we cautiously ventured beyond Mrs. Tibbs, the hefty crossing guard, Buzz and Jimmy lurked silently in the shadows, ready to pounce on us when we least expected it. Lana and I lived three blocks from school, but it felt like three miles. Buzz and Jimmy had a system. They ripped off our backpacks in a New York minute and dumped the contents at their feet. Loose change, *Tootsie rolls*, colored pencils, and Cracker Jack prizes fell to the ground. All of our cherished possessions were fair game. The twins were so quick, even eagle-eyed Mrs. Tibbs could not incriminate them. Lana and I sadly limped home, candy-less and penniless. Monsters, Boogie Men, and the *Big Bad Wolf* were tame in comparison to the nightmare I faced every night when I closed my eyes to sleep. I could picture Buzz and Jimmy's evil freckle-filled faces ridiculing me, mocking and mean.

As a sheltered, spoiled little girl, the world was cold and hard. Bullies, neighborhood dogs, thunder, and cranky Mr. Gardner down the street caused my heart to pause and skip a beat. However, as I reflect upon these villains in my past, my perspective has altered somewhat. I have a theory. Every evil little thug knew for a fact that grade-school girls were creepy and should be shunned. "She-monsters" were expert tattlers, and female teachers often gave little boy classmates the benefit of the slop. In their own way, little girls could be catty and vicious, like Chihuahuas nipping relentlessly at someone's heels. Principal Moffett always paddled (yes, paddled) errant boys, but girls always got to plea bargain for inside information on classroom pranks.

Young boys of our day were told to idolize football heroes like Mean Joe Green and Johnny Unitas—men who raked in millions of dollars for pulverizing each other on the football field. A cartoon hero like Wiley Coyote was heralded as clever for procuring Acme dynamite, anvils, and booby traps to annihilate the Roadrunner. Tom and Jerry whacked each other with croquet mallets, and we were supposed to join in the fun. Christmas presents for boys always included guns and swords.

Male machismo was the order of the day, and little boys weren't supposed to cry. Girl-clobbering might simply be a cover to mask the pain of a dad who didn't come home or a mom who never listened. Perhaps the classroom menace often felt a lonely ache deep inside. As I reflect upon the tough exterior that present-day bullies wear, I often find a gooey-cream center beneath the hard-candy exterior. The next time I face one, I'll try a little tenderness.

> *There is no fear in love. But perfect love drives out fear, because fear has to do with punishment. The one who fears is not made perfect in love. We love because he first loved us. If anyone says, "I love God," yet hates his brother, he is a liar. For anyone who does not love*

his brother, whom he has seen, cannot love God, whom he has not seen. And he has given us this command: Whoever loves God must also love his brother. (1 John 4:18–21 NIV)

Paraphrase these verses in your own words.

What insight do you gain from this promise?

How would you describe "perfect love"? Where does this kind of love come from?

According to John, how is loving others connected to loving God?

Spend some time with God, asking Him to give you a forgiving heart toward your enemies.

Queen Of Everything
The Perils Of Pride

God's blessings in our lives can easily be turned into smug, self-satisfied arrogance if we grab the glory for ourselves, rather than thanking Him and giving Jesus His well-deserved honor and worship. Climbing the ladder of success led to a well-deserved serving of humble pie for me.

My fifth grade year was absotively, posolutely the best year of my life. Everything went downhill from there. Those were the days: pre-glasses, pre-braces, and pre-trans-fats. Mrs. Douglas was my teacher, and I was unequivocally her precious pet. She sported a "bubble-cut" hairdo beautifully plastered with Dep Hair Gel and always dressed in neon clothes. I adored her, and the feeling was mutual. Every time Mrs. D. posed a question, my hand shot up like a rocket and I pontificated about any subject we studied, whether I knew the right answer or not. My classmates were mildly annoyed, but they didn't persecute me as much as I deserved.

The School Spelling Bee was held every October like clock-work. With my newfound confidence as class genius, I determined to add another star to my crown. I would take on Elma Studder, the two-time seventh grade spelling champion, and grind her to a pulp. I poured over the bee study book in the bathtub, during recess, and even during *Lassie*.

The big day arrived. We faced off like two ornery gunslingers. Elma pulled out her Colt 45 and aced "beneficent." I fired back with "anonymous." After a heated exchange, I obliterated her with "zygote." "Zygote. Z-y-g-o-t-e. Zygote." The seventh grade students were horrified. Elma was their pride and joy. How could a smart-mouthed fifth grader de-throne her? Maybe she didn't eat her Wheaties that morning…maybe my steely stare unnerved her. I gloated over her defeat.

I now proudly seized my throne as Queen Bee. The newspaperman took my picture (fuzzy ponytail, pot belly and all), and I grinned like a Cheshire cat. Even Betsy the crossing guard quaked in her Keds upon my approach. I hesitate to mention I was shot down on the first word of the District Spelling Bee. "Independence. I-n-d-e-p-e-n-d-a-n-c-e. Independance." What was I thinking?

Even my district defeat couldn't snuff out my euphoria. My spelling bee fame won the heart of Phil Taylor, the blue-eyed boy with the buzz cut in math class. Phil fell madly in love with me. He scrawled a note in homeroom asking me to be princess of the Oak Cliff Nuggets, his Little League softball team. My chest swelled (s-w-e-l-l-e-d) with pride. Mom bought me a new ruffly dress and some grown-up lady undergarments. She twisted my hair into a bun and let me wear a smidgen of her racy red lip balm. Phil and his teammates presented me with a 50-cent silver tiara. I knew I was a dead ringer for Marilyn Monroe (no pun intended). I held court on the school playground and smugly lorded my royal position over my "peon" girlfriends.

Parade day arrived. Spring had sprung and softball season had just gotten into swing. Phil and I proudly perched on top of the back seat of a pink *Cadillac* convertible. The four-car Little League parade crept down Jefferson Street. It didn't matter that the only onlookers were our doting parents. I proudly practiced my gloved beauty queen wave: elbow-elbow-wrist-wrist. It was uncool for beauty queens to look excited. Princesses always appeared blasé, even bored with their adoring fans. After signing autographs (one for my Grandma and one for my little sister, Kathy), Phil and I sauntered over to the softball field. I had no idea what a foul ball or a strike was. I had never even witnessed a softball game, so I simply continued my beauty queen wave and sucked down my *Dr. Pepper*.

The Nuggets had a rough year. Their heavy-hitter, Barney Lampson, dislocated his shoulder in a backyard brawl. A foul ball in the second game of the season clipped Arnie Smith, the catcher. Onlookers were mostly parents, and they were lathered up in a frenzy, yelling advice to the players. The prospects for winning the pennant were bleak. But this was my moment to shine. I would not be the poster-girl for a losing team! I saved up my allowance money and bought three pairs of red crepe paper pom-poms. My girlfriends, Lana and Laura, joined my cheerleading squad. Even though the Nuggets were downhearted, we lifted their spirits and cheered them on to victory. By April, Nugget players and parent celebrated their hard-won victory by polishing off five pepperoni pizzas at *Pizza Hut*. Even though I had no athletic prowess, I was certain MY cheer squad lifted the Nuggets out of the doldrums and skyrocketed them to victory.

I was unstoppable. I was insufferable to my sister Kathy, I snubbed my buddies, and I bragged until my buttons burst. My winning streak continued. I should have bought a lottery ticket. Of course, the Tackers were good Baptists, and gambling was taboo. I still think I could have made a killing. Once again I triumphed, this time in the culinary department. Every April, the PTA held a chili cook-off. Each student was required to concoct a version of the greasy soup. We simmered spices to create just the right combination of *Tabasco* and ground meat. Parents were not allowed to help. I started by filling my stew pot with *Heinz ketchup*. I also dumped in a bottle of *Heinz 57* — a high-quality condiment. I spared no expense — no cheap generic ingredients would do. Then I simmered the meat for an eternity — at least thirty minutes. I watched Julia Child on TV and she always added beer to everything, so I sneaked next door to my Methodist neighbors and borrowed a can of *Budweiser*. The sauce still needed some zing, so I chopped six fresh jalapeno peppers and five onions. My soup could peel paint. Believe it or not, "Julie's chili" was a hit. The blue ribbon is still on my refrigerator. To this day, it is the only thing I can cook without poisoning my family.

After a satisfying spring, my final triumphant moment came in May, just before the school year ended. Mr. Carpenter, our somewhat effeminate choir teacher, selected Stephanie Burkett, Ronald Palmer and me to sing in the cherub chorus of *Boito's Requiem* with the Dallas Symphony Orchestra. Each afternoon, we warbled our parts with Mr. Carpenter. Our Italian pronunciation was impeccable. Stephanie, Ronald, and I became the rock stars of the music class. We even had our own entourage. Boito was an Italian composer obsessed with the afterlife. Dressed as heavenly cherubs, we three perched in the Music Hall balcony with 97 other little angels and chirped out our three-stanza Italian phrases. I can still remember the words. I can't remember my social security number, but I can sing *"Fra telli per namci lontano fin ultimo cielo non tano, poi sempre dove angelo cantar."* Maestro Johanos artfully pointed his baton toward us and we warbled like nightingales.

The cherub chorus balcony was in the nosebleed section of the concert hall. We could barely see the violinists. Our angel army was crammed together like sardines, and the overhead spotlights beat down upon our sweaty foreheads. Soon the ammonia from our perspiration made Tommy Ligdorf a little queasy. Tommy, third row, sixth seat from the left, had contracted the stomach flu shortly before our debut. He spewed his dinner all over the altos before we sang the first "Fratelli..." Once Stephanie saw Tommy toss his cookies, she hurled her undigested French fries into the tuba below. A few fragments landed on the tenors in hell (the orchestra pit). Bedlam ensued. In spite of a somewhat rocky start, the concert went off without a hitch. Maestro Johanos was from Moscow, and Russians are not easily ruffled. We receive a standing ovation, and I had my cherub robe bronzed for posterity. (Just kidding).

My fame was proclaimed from the rooftops — by *moi*, of course! But celebrity is short-lived. Elma Studder reclaimed the spelling bee trophy the next fall with a dazzling *antidisestablishmentarianism*. I pooped out on *laboratory*. Phil Taylor, my enamored suitor, jilted me for a freckle-faced redhead named Lacey in math class. My luck with men didn't improve until my freshman year in college. The Dallas Symphony has yet to call me back for "cherub duty." Rats.

I finally saw all of the hoopla for what it was — fleeting and fading. I needed a dose of reality therapy, and God graciously gave it to me. But my come-uppance turned out to be a blessing. He showed me who I truly am — His forgiven daughter, a wife and mother and a grateful servant of my Lord.

"Pride brings a person low, but the lowly in spirit gain honor. (Proverbs 29:23 NIV)
"Pride lands you flat on your face; humility prepares you for honors." (Proverbs 29:23 The Message)

List some synonyms for pride. What does a proud person look like? Why would pride sabotage relationships?

Has your pride ever hurt those closest to you? When? Did you find healing when you humbled yourself before God and those whom you had injured?

Spend some time thinking of ways you can build others up. The next time you are with a friend, try listening patiently rather than talking and "tooting your own horn." Making others feel valued and respected can be deeply rewarding. Ask God to help you do this today.

Chores
Dirty Duties

What do you get when you combine a potty brush, Mr. Clean, a ratty rag and a HAZ-MAT suit? Weekly chores! Chores have no redeeming value for kids. I'd rather be horsewhipped than don my potty-cleaning garb. Weekly housecleaning duties came out of nowhere. One minute I was sitting on the couch, mindlessly chomping potato chips, and the next minute I was forced into hard labor.

"Chore" Saturday started after my first week of school. My friend, Lana, told me that school would be fun. Boy, was she wrong! I was so excited to go to first grade instead of lame old kindergarten. So my first school day, I jumped out of bed before the sun came up. I sat patiently while Mommy untangled the rats in my freshly permed hair. I pulled my lacy white socks on all by myself and stepped into my itchy new plaid jumper and crisp white shirt. I even helped Mommy make my lunch by spreading *Miracle Whip* on my *Bumble*

Bee tuna sandwich. As I approached the school blacktop, I held my breath, forced a smile and sucked in my stomach to meet the new kids.

Nobody told me I had to attend school for FIVE DAYS every week for TWELVE YEARS. Unbelievable! I was flabbergasted. Elementary school had no naps and no snack time. How are we supposed to survive without a little sleep and sugar each afternoon? I was bummed. When I returned from school, I pouted, plopped my feet on the furniture in rebellion, and left my leftover sandwich to rot in my lunch box. I sulked and watched *Tom and Jerry* pulverize each other with rubber mallets. I knew just how they felt. At least Jerry could escape to his rat hole.

I, on the other hand, woke up bleary-eyed at the crack of dawn, sucked down my Malt-O-Meal and mindlessly brushed my bicuspids morning after morning. The same hair-untangling ritual ensued day after day. (I must have been a violent sleeper.) Mom shoved my backpack in my hand and I dutifully dragged myself down the street toward the schoolyard.

How could school be such a drag? Didn't I learn everything I needed to learn on the first day? I already knew my alphabet, I could count to one hundred, and I could sign my name with a smiley-face. What other survival skills would I need to marry a rich oil tycoon and settle down in the 'burbs? Days grew into weeks: Wednesday's lukewarm Sloppy Joe lunch, Thursday's rainy-day dodge ball match, and Friday's lukewarm fish stick meal were old hat by October.

One ray of hope made the whole ordeal bearable: slug-a-bed Saturdays! During my cushy kindergarten days, Saturdays were like heaven. I could stay up late on Friday night, gorging on popcorn and pulling my sister's ponytail. I slept in until nine a.m. and woke up to Aunt Jemima pancakes slathered in butter and Mrs. Butterworth's syrup. After stuffing my face, I parked on a lime green beanbag chair and watched cartoons until lunchtime, bloated and burping from my pancake binge. Saturday afternoons were filled with tricycle riding, ladybug hunting, and mud-pie baking. All of my cherished pastimes came to a screeching halt when Mom and Dad sentenced me to hard labor. "You are a big girl now, Julie," they said. "It's time for you to learn to be responsible." I was concerned. The word "responsible" had an unpleasant ring to it.

Parents instituted "Chores" to be sure that all of the fun and adventure were sucked out of life. Dolly-dressing was replaced by bed-making. Sister-chasing was turned into trash-taking. Late-sleeping became floor-sweeping. My folks justified their demands by promising an "allowance" for performing these disgusting duties. But two nickels and a dime were small compensation for these indignities, especially since Kathy and I could rummage through the couch cushions and find pocket change for ourselves.

Mom said chores would keep us out of jail when we became grownups. "Learning to apply a little elbow grease," she said, "will keep you from turning into a wino or a bank-robber." Thus the ritual Saturday scouring became a dreaded weekly event.

Boys always had it better than girls when it came to chores. Dougie Scott, my next door buddy, got to hop on a riding mower and pretend to be a roughshod, rabble-rousing cowboy roaming the range. Occasionally, he had to sweep the garage, but the cement floor was a treasure trove of washers, screws, and squiggly bugs. Good times. His little brother, Donnie, got to hop on his bike and pedal down to the A & P to buy laundry detergent. His mom (a saint, in my estimation) put a nickel in his pocket for a Slim Jim to compensate him for his time and trouble.

Girl chores were the worst! I discovered that if I closed my eyes and held my nose, I could make a few swipes at the toilet bowl rim. The submerged brush might or might not dislodge the icky goo near the flushing hole. If worse came to worst, I plunged my rubber glove into the brackish water and gave a quick swish to complete the task. My mom always came for "flush" inspection, and if the loo didn't make the grade, I had to start all over again. That's why I am a certifiable germaphobe today.

Folding my dad's clean pants and my sister's tee shirts were no problem. I pretended to be wrapping Christmas presents, and they folded nicely and neatly. But boxer briefs and petticoats were much more challenging. I squished them in a ball and shoved them into the bottom drawer when my mom wasn't looking. Fitted sheet folding was the worst. Where were the corners, where was the middle? I sat on the cotton puffs to crease them flat and finally gave up. So I popped the elastic sheet corner over my head and ran through the house, pretending to be *Casper the Friendly Ghost* (Fitted sheets were also perfect for non-slip wedding veils!)

My last and most harrowing task was "corner patrol." I shoved a dishrag full of Mr. Clean under the fridge, behind the closet doors, and under the bed, dissolving dust bunnies, spider webs, and dirty Kleenex in every nook and cranny of our abode. Friday night was filled with nightmares about snakes and tarantulas that might burst forth to attack me when I bothered their Frigidaire lair.

My little sister, Kathy, got all the cushy chores. She was given a cute little red oven mitt to "dust" the furniture. She flitted all around the house, pretending to spread "fairy dust." The problem with dusting is that it is totally ineffective. One simply moves the dust to another location. Mommy snickered and turned a blind eye to the fingerprinted streaky coffee table. Oh, the injustice of it all! Dusting took about ten minutes. Potty duty took ten years (or at least it felt that way.) After suffering the indignity of toilet duty, my next job was taking out the trash. Trash duty, before the days of trash can liners, involved pre-chewed gum scraping and snotty Kleenex removal.

Bed-making was also Kathy's job, but since she was too little to run around and crease the corners, Mommy always helped her. (I always knew Mommy loved Kathy best!) The only way I could annoy Sissy was to make those fitted sheets so wrinkly that she had to spend at least five extra minutes sheet smoothing.

Kathy's last assignment was shoe-arranging. (Is that even a real job?) She wasn't responsible for arranging anyone else's footwear— just her own. For as long as I can remember, Kathy was a die-hard shoe hog. In preschool, she pitched a fit in *Sears* if Mom didn't buy her some *Keds* with sparkly toes. By second grade, she begged Mom to spring for the newest pink t-strap flats. By high school, Kathy was working at Shoe Heaven and spending her entire salary on inventory. Now her shoe closet looks like Jessica Simpson's. Yep, for Kathy, shoe arranging was no chore at all. Unfair, I say, unfair!

The sister discrimination also extended to kitchen duties. As the older sister, I had to learn how to prepare the main dishes like pot roast. Kathy got to bake cookies and ice cakes. While I had no desire to eat the mushroom soup or sample the raw onions, Kathy feasted on raw cookie dough, warm cookie crumbs, and icing-covered butter knives. To this day, Kathy is a pastry chef and I get creative with *Jell-O* and *Cool Whip*. But I make a mean *Hamburger Helper*.

My older sister jealousy and pent-up aggression dissipated by noon, just in time for *McNuggets* and a strawberry *Slurpee*. At least half a Saturday was better than no Saturday at all. As I look back on my early conscription into *choredom*, I discovered a disturbing but universal truth. Chores are about growing up. Every adult spends much of his or her life doing jobs they absolutely hate! No mom wants to clean a poopy diaper, but she suffers the stench because she loves her baby. No dad wants to bandage a gooey, bloody knee scrape (unless he's a surgeon or a vampire), but he does it because he loves his clumsy son.

God said taking care of humans is like taking care of smelly sheep. It is definitely A CHORE. Sheep never mind, they get lost, and they are positively un-trainable. They fall over and can't get up, and they are scared of their own shadows. So how does God put up with us, His clueless little sheep? He does it because He is the Good Shepherd and gladly lays down His life for His little flock.

> *11 "I am the good shepherd. The good shepherd lays down his life for the sheep. 12 A hired hand will run when he sees a wolf coming. He will leave the sheep because they aren't his and he isn't their shepherd. And so the wolf attacks them and scatters the flock. 13 The hired hand runs away because he is merely hired and has no real concern for the sheep. 14 "I am the good shepherd; I know my own sheep, and they know me, 15 just as my Father knows me and I know the Father. And I lay down my life for the sheep."* (John 10:11-15 NIV)

Jesus describes Himself as the Good Shepherd. What are the "chores" of the shepherd? How does He care for His sheep? Who is the hired hand? Why is he negligent about his "shepherd duties"? Contrast the work of the Good Shepherd and the hired hand.

What are some ways you can guard and protect those God has placed in your care? Is loving others a chore or a delight? Why or why not? Ask God to give you the heart of a faithful shepherd.

As believers, Jesus said we hear the voice of the Shepherd and follow Him. Have you heard His voice? Think about the wonderful gift of a God who would lay down His life for you. Spend some time meditating on that great gift, and give Him thanks for His sacrifice.

Sitter Babies
The Wardens Are Coming

Mommy and Daddy definitely needed a break from yours truly. Although I was adorable beyond words, my clever antics often caused my parents stress and consternation. The day Daddy threatened to phone "Happy Day Sanitarium" to order a strait jacket for Mom, they both decided to implement emergency measures to ensure their survival. Not only did they wrestle with me from dawn to dusk, but a new "bundle of joy" (Who says?) came to live at the Tacker house. Baby sister Kathy was also quite a handful, kicking and screaming like a banshee.

Mommy was on her last nerve. I wasn't sure what pushed her over the edge. Was it my Houdini escapes out of the front door into oncoming traffic? Was it my science experiments flushing pencils, watches, and Julia the Cat down the toilet? Was it my fascination with all things sharp, poisonous or electrical? Who could be sure?

After much deliberation and a few bottles of Jack Daniels (just kidding), my parents concluded that a babysitter would provide them with a much-needed reprieve from the whirlwind that was me. However, they were unaware that babysitters came in all shapes and sizes: the good, the bad, and the ugly. Caretakers for their offspring weren't always reliable.

"Sitter babies" were the most readily available choice. A "sitter baby" was a thirteen-year-old tweener girl who aggravated her parents so much that her "tweener mommy" hocked her for hire to perturb some other family. "Sitter Baby" Buffy Blankenship shuffled through the door, mumbled "hello," and proceeded to hog the remote and telephone every boy in her seventh grade class. The "sitter baby" we encountered was selfish and immature. Buffy never let us win at *checkers* or *Yahtzee*, and forgot to flush the toilet or feed us supper. She put her feet on the furniture and yelled at us incessantly. Buffy was the big sister from hell, and I always rejoiced when she left.

"Beanie Babysitter" was a slovenly slug who lived on our cul-de-sac. Ernie Schillings was a hard-core couch potato. He parked himself on the sofa and played fetch with me. "Fetch the cold pizza," he grunted. "Fetch the root beer." "Fetch the marshmallow creme." Before I could protest, he seized the *Nintendo* joystick and never looked my way again. Baby sister Kathy happily cooed in her infant seat, perched on a pile of poop, unnoticed by Ernie. Mom returned, horrified by the potato chip-encrusted couch and the empty frig. For some reason, "Beanie Babysitter" Ernie never returned. I think he spent the next two years rotting in juvy.

"Cry Babysitter" always kept score. Fifteen-year-old Angela Tooksberry had a knack for incessant criticism. She kept score all night. If I whined, she told. If I threw my toys, she tattled. If I poked Kathy in her high chair, she snitched. Time out was purgatory when "Cry Babysitter" Tooksberry was in charge. A tortured soul, I spent many an evening rotting in the corner of the living room, awaiting the wrath of my returning parent. Nothing escaped "Cry Babysitter's" withering glance. Moving violations, sister-needling, and checker-cheating were all painstakingly recorded. My wall of shame was posted on the refrigerator door. Every evil act was re-lived when I went to forage for a *Popsicle* or yellow *Jell-O*. Daddy was reminded of my sins when he opened the icebox door to drink from the milk carton (an unpardonable sin by my germaphobe mother's standards). Everyone was glad to see "Cry Babysitter" Tooksbury leave and take her pointy, accusing finger with her.

"Sly Sitter" Martha English took advantage of inside intel to get what she wanted. Martha played the responsible sixteen-year-old in order to nab my parent's car keys. She threw us in the back seat of our *Chevy Chevette* and cranked the radio until the car shook. The Chevy was a hot convertible, so Martha donned her imitation *Versace* sunglasses and trolled the main drag of Kiest Park, looking for boys. Bad boys. We loved drag-racing and boy-chasing with "Sly Sitter." She knew where Mom's mad money was stashed and pilfered enough to buy *Seventeen* magazines and rum raisin ice cream from the Polar Bear Ice Cream palace. Martha lounged on the hood of our sports coupe and let us play in parking lot puddles until dinnertime. We spent many mischievous afternoons with Martha, our ponytails flapping in the breeze. Once Mom saw us careening down the highway with Martha's latest boyfriend, Rocko, "Sly Sitter" was history.

After Martha was canned, Mommy was desperate. "Senile Sitter," crochety old Mrs. Turkle from next door, filled in the gap between babysitters. Turkle had a soft spot for my mom. So when "Sly Sitter" disappeared with her tattooed boyfriend, "Senile Sitter" came to the rescue. Turkle reluctantly turned off "Wheel of Fortune" and padded over to our house in her muu-muu and Hush Puppy slippers. Once Mom and Dad peeled out of the driveway, "Senile Sitter" switched on the boob tube and snored like a freight train until the nightly news was done. With sleepy Turkle, Kathy and I had the run of the house. We polished off three boxes of *Pop Tarts*. We poured *Suave* shampoo into Daddy's loafers, we scrawled our names on the bathroom mirror with Mommy's peach passion lipstick, and we drew an exceptional mural on the hallway wall with colored chalk. When Turkle was on duty, all bets were off. I guess that's why "Senile Sitter" was not called again. It took Mom three days to dig through the wreckage and repaint the hallway.

At long last, "Super Sitter" came into our lives! Joni Milner spent her last two semesters in home economics taking mommy lessons and watching way too many reruns of *Mary Poppins*. Joni was "practically perfect in every way." "Super Sitter" cheerily rapped upon our front door one summer morning, burst into the living room wearing a freshly pressed white blouse, plaid skirt, and penny loafers. She pulled out a scented resume replete with first aid certification, character references, and an honor roll sticker. When "Super Sitter" Joni was around, bedtime was early, vegetables were consumed, and manners were mandatory. Earwax and boogers were extracted and toenails were clipped. You'd think we had visited the dog groomer. TV dinners were of the devil, according to Joni. No *Vienna sausages*, *Chef Boy-ar-Dee ravioli* or bologna sandwiches would touch our lips. Approved snacks included celery sticks and cheese strings. Joni cooked from scratch and our lunches were hot, yummy, and homemade. She carefully cut the crusts off of our tuna sandwiches. Our usual summer tummy paunch flattened. We even had rosy cheeks!

Joni was always prompt, chipper and reliable. She always brought a "surprise sack" to her babysitting gigs. One night, the "surprise sack" contained a sock puppet named Arnold and a pack of pipe cleaners. Kathy was thrilled! She used the sock puppet to hurl all the insults that she didn't have the guts to say to my face without wooly footwear on her hand. I retaliated by poking her in the belly button with the pipe cleaners. I don't think Joni envisioned her "surprises" being used in this way. But "Super Sitter" was resourceful. She pulled out the play dough and blew up balloon animals. We were captivated. We slipped off to sleep happy and well-fed. Yep, Joni was a keeper.

In fact, Joni was a bridesmaid at my wedding. Now that's "staying power"!

> *¹ I lift up my eyes to the mountains—*
>
>   *where does my help come from?*
>
> *² My help comes from the LORD,*
>
>   *the Maker of heaven and earth.*
>
> *³ He will not let your foot slip—*
>
>   *he who watches over you will not slumber;*
>
> *⁴ indeed, he who watches over Israel*
>
>   *will neither slumber nor sleep.*
>
> *⁵ The LORD watches over you—*
>
>   *the LORD is your shade at your right hand;*
>
> *⁶ the sun will not harm you by day,*
>
>   *nor the moon by night.*
>
> *⁷ The LORD will keep you from all harm—*
>
>   *he will watch over your life;*
>
> *⁸ the LORD will watch over your coming and going*
>
>   *both now and forevermore.* (Psalm 121:1-8 NIV)

God is the "Super Sitter" in this psalm, one of the psalms of ascents written to assure traveling pilgrims of God's protection

on their journey to Jerusalem. In verses 3-8, the poet recounts the ways God watches over His children. List them here.

How does it make you feel to know that God never goes to sleep? He lovingly answers prayers while you are snoring away. How many times is the word "watching" used in this psalm? What does it tell you about its importance? Tonight, when you are drifting off, picture God as a vigilant sentinel guarding you from danger and enemies

From what do you need protection in these verses? What are some dangers and temptations that you face? Write them here. Spend some time praying for God's protecting hand in your life. Thank Him for being a "Super Sitter."

Van Gogh and Fish Guts

Tacker family outings were diverse, to say the least. They either involved brush strokes or fish guts. My dad, dubbed Ralph Murle by his father, Ralph Waldo, had a lot to overcome in the name department. Nicknames or initials were a must for him to avoid incessant playground ridicule. (My mom's name was "Wanda Lanier" — a weird moniker as well.) Thank God I didn't have an ancestral label to incite teasing during my elementary school days!

But with a name like "Ralph Murle," my dad had much to defend. Thankfully, he was up for the challenge. A wild child from preschool days, I have been told he pretended to be *Tarzan*, swinging from a pecan tree branch with a butcher knife in his mouth. Little Ralphie scampered up the telephone pole and tried to walk the electric tightrope like a circus performer. His mom tanned his hide. How he managed to keep his appendages intact is still an unsolved mystery. Ralph mischievously pilfered his beautiful older sister's chocolate-covered cherries and painstakingly poked holes in the bottom of each gooey morsel. These and other elaborate misadventures helped Ralph Murle overcome his quirky name. From a colorful post-war childhood emerged a man who was half-country and half-city boy.

Dad's interests were broad — to say the least. He was a brilliant artist, a poet, and a potter. He also was a down-to-earth fisherman smelling of perspiration and minnows. Some of my earliest childhood escapades were spent trekking through art museums or casting for trout. Kathy and I traipsed through the *Dallas Art Museum* sporting our zebra-striped jingle-bell sneakers. The museum police hated our jingle-belling in the presence of *Van Gogh's* irises and *Monet's* cathedrals. They believed such masters deserved silent reverence and awe. We thought the artists would appreciate our happy, tinkly choreography. I could identify a *Rembrandt* before I could ride a two-wheeler.

Kathy and I loved to play hide 'n seek in the sculpture wing of the art museum. We played "tag-you're it" by *Rodin's "The Thinker"* (a copy, by the way) and pretended Mr. Thinker was constipated. He probably ordered the fried cheese sticks from the museum café. That will do it every time. We loved to suck our stomachs in and stand frozen beside *Venus de Milo*. We copied her armless pose and hoped one day to be as shapely as she. Other sculptures were more abstract — bicycles welded to lawnmowers and golf clubs to represent the angst of modern life. I stood on my head to see if I could understand what the artist was trying to portray and came up empty every time.

His nagging wife probably asked him to clean out the garage, so he welded it all together and called it art.

The museum security guards were fairly tolerant of Kathy and me, since our family had season passes, but they finally tired of our sock-sliding through the Flemish painter gallery. The somber portraits looked down at us with consternation and disgust. Busted!!! The art police marched us over to Mom and Dad, who stood perplexed in front of *Picasso's "Lady in Blue."* "Did she have two heads or three?" they mused. "Was that her belly button or her ear?" Who could tell? Our house arrest cut short our family's little outing. Ralph and Wanda grabbed us by the nape of the neck and marched us toward the door. What a shame...the museum was air-conditioned and our house was not. The bathroom floors were marble, and the bookstore sported an endless supply of postcards and pop-up books. Even with our abrupt exit, we promised Mom and Dad we would behave better next time. Thus, our museum afternoons were a regular part of our summer fun.

The "fishing trips" were glorious fun for Daddy. Mom, being madly in love with Ralph Murle, tolerated his love for all things fishy. Kathy and I dutifully went along for the ride. We were rousted out of bed in the middle of the night (about four a.m.) and deposited in the back seat of the car. Apparently the fish on *Lake Tawakoni* were early risers. During the long ride to the lake, Kathy and I dreamt a lazier Saturday morning filled with cartoons and *Toast-em'*

Pop Ups. The only redeeming part of our lake expedition was the hot home-fried donut holes at the live bait shop.

The Tacker angling ritual ensued, despite our protests. Lures, lines, rods, and reels were carefully laid out and counted like weapons in an arsenal used to defeat an aquatic enemy. My job was to be sure the fishing line did not get tangled. Then it got ugly. Out came the jar of muddy, bloody earthworms destined to be skewered on the fish-hooks. Perky little minnows also faced serious body-piercing before they were tossed into the murky water. (Or we assumed it was water. How could you tell in the dark?) The pitiful little creatures awaited the bite of a menacing trout or bass. After hook-hanging and fish-snagging, the "live bait" didn't stay alive for long. The whole process seemed gory and barbaric to my way of thinking. However, getting a wiggly fish on the line wasn't too bad. We'd scoop the little fishies into a net and let them off the hook (or so they thought). Their tiny little fish brains never anticipated they were heading for a fiery pan to be fried, poached, or baked with some catsup and finger-licking hush puppies.

Bait fishing was brutish, but fly fishing was pretty entertaining for a kid. Shiny feather-filled lures and swimmers were tethered to the end of the fishing line. After a quick snap of the wrist, the lure sailed over our heads and landed "plunkety plunk" in the water. We quietly, carefully reeled in the fishing line in hopes of snagging a big one. Occasionally, a particularly stupid bass forgot the piece of metal in the water was not real food and grabbed the lure with his large, bony mouth. Tugging and reeling in the fish was quite a rush! The only hazard of fly-fishing was casting backlash. Chaos reigned when I pulled the hook and line too far behind my head and hooked the seat of my pants. Occasionally I hooked my sister's ponytail. Not a good idea. This snafu occurred at least once on fly fishing Saturdays.

Fishing was not like "museuming." We were sweaty, the lake was stinky and mosquito-ridden, and if we needed to pee, Daddy told us to jump off the boat and go in the lake. For a boy, this was a simple task, but for a little girl this was total commitment. I would rather pull one of my eyes out of its socket than jump in that murky water. How many other people had used the lake for this purpose? Beer cans and leftover bologna sandwiches floated past. Cotton-mouthed rattlers were rumored to slither through the water. Kathy and I hollered for a real bathroom until Daddy puttered over to the dock and let us use the *Texaco* ladies room. He was perturbed and longed for boys who weren't so particular about such things.

Fishing excursions came to a close when the sun rose high in the sky. Fish swam deeper to catch their mid-afternoon naps. Unlike the trout, our fun had only begun. Daddy proceeded to teach us the fine art of "skinning" the fish. Between the lake and the lunch table existed a malodorous process of decapitating the prey — their glassy eyes staring you in the face and their tails still flopping. Then the fisherman (or fisher-girls, in our case) took a fistful of fish guts and ripped them out of the poor little trout's body without anesthesia. As a final insult, all of the fish bones were removed, and the iron skillet was fired to red-hot. This little fishy would be hotter than hell. Kathy and I felt like cannibals. We named each little crapi we caught. Who were we eating? Wally, Harold, or Nemo? I guess you probably ascertained which outing I preferred — the museum was far and away my favorite. Fishing was a necessary evil to keep Daddy happy for the rest of the week.

However, my sister taught me a very important lesson. Instead of complaining on lake day, she went willingly just to enjoy the look of delight on my father's face. Kathy knew she was entering her father's world and that it greatly blessed his heart to share his fishy hobby. Kathy probably did not enjoy lake day any more than I did, but she faithfully joined him in his love of angling. As she grew up and became a mom, her children watched in amazement as Grandpa baited, hooked, and cooked. My daughters loved the *Louvre*, but Kathy's kids also loved the lake.

> *"This is how we know what love is: Jesus Christ laid down His life for us. And we ought to lay down our lives for our brothers. ...Dear children, let u not love with words or tongue but with actions and in truth."* (1 John 3:16-18 NIV)

Jesus' love for us was demonstrated by laying down His life for others. One definition of attention is entering the world of

another person. Is there someone you love whose interests are far different than yours? Can you think of some ways you can lovingly lay down your own interests, your own life, to "enter their world" and be excited about their passions and perspectives? List them here.

Christ's model for servanthood and humility is pictured in this passage. Read the verses carefully and list the ways Jesus deferred His own needs to lay down His life for us. After reading this passage, think of a time when you spoke loving words and also demonstrated loving actions as well.

What would loving someone by not "demanding your own way" look like with your family? Think of someone you know who is humble, patient and unselfish. List instances where these qualities were displayed. What can you learn from them?

Tea Parties
Yogi and Arf-Arf

Tea parties are part of a little girl's DNA, along with dress-up and boy hating. My earliest tea soirees consisted of my baby blankie, Yogi the teddy bear, and Arf-Arf, my stuffed beagle. The fare was simple — baby bottles full of water and dried prunes. Mom determined that only dried fruit snack spills would come out of my bubble-gum pink bedroom carpet. Yogi and Arf-Arf were water-soaked, but the prunes kept them regular.

When Kathy, my little sister, entered the picture, the tea parties became more elaborate affairs. I had to bribe her with real food to induce her to play. Milk and cookies were on the menu, and Barbie, Skipper, and Midge were the esteemed guests. Our only male doll, Ken, was never invited. He spent most of his days lonely and naked in the toy box. Ken couldn't wear evening dresses or rubber high heels like Barbie (at least not in those days), so he remained in solitary confinement, only to make an appearance as the occasional dream date or groom. Kathy was younger than I, so I forced her to "be Ken" — a humiliating job when playing pretend.

Now, back to the party plans. We scoured the house for the perfect location. A bed sheet covered the dining room table and satin pillows were surreptitiously absconded from the living room couch. The milk was filled with strawberry Quik, and we stuffed Fig Newtons down our throats lickety-split. Barbie and Midge refused to eat because they were always dieting to prevent their perfect little plastic bodies from collecting cellulite. Barbie, created in 1964, is still in impeccable shape. If you see her in the toy aisle, nothing droops, wrinkles, pooches, or freckles. She is forever flawless and ageless. I hate her.

By kindergarten, tea parties included our little play-date girl-friends: Susie, Sandy, and Hilda. We hated inviting Hilda because she always inhaled the refreshments before we were finished setting the table and toting the dollies. "Real girl" tea parties were usually full of drama. Little girls, like big girls, have a natural pecking order. The loudest and bossiest guest, usually Sandy, got the first dolly pick and the *Teddy Grahams*. Shy Susie was lucky to get *Pitiful Pearl* and a crumbled vanilla wafer. "Real girl" tea parties often started well, but devolved into "my dolly is bigger than your dolly" fights. Mom banished everyone to their own homes and made us take a nap — a cruel fate for a five-year-old.

My momma understood our fascination with tea celebrations. Growing up on a dirt farm in East Texas was hard for my mom.

Grandpa and Grandma B barely eked out a living for their tiny family. Everybody worked day and night to plant, harvest, and can the food they ate. Her parents couldn't afford many toys, so Grandma B created dollies from corn husks and scraps of cloth. Momma never owned a china doll, but these little companions fashioned with love were precious to her. The crude little corn husk girls gathered in the corner of the living room next to the coal-covered fireplace. Tea sets were costly, so Grandma B gave her little tot the cracked cups that were no longer usable for morning coffee. Mommy was an only child, so the friends who gathered around her tea table were imaginary. But she had an elegant tablecloth—a doily my Granny had artfully crocheted with white thread and little blue beads. Mom cherishes that lacy treasure to this day.

Those were her childhood tea-totaling days. As a grownup, Mom worked as the accountant for Dad's business, so Saturday was our special day together. Saturday morning did not seem special at first glance. Mom marched us down to the kitchen, shoved a bowl of Cream of Wheat (it tasted like paste) down our gullets, and passed out the cleaning supplies. We dutifully performed our morning chores, knowing that there was fun to be had when we finished our tasks. After all, Momma knew how to work hard. So her little charges were required to "earn" their fun before teatime began. Our happy "tea outings" did not come without a price. But it was worth the effort!

You can imagine the delight my mom had at treating her little girls to a tea party in grand style... Saturday's activities were not simply relegated to cooking and cleaning. At noon, Mom blew the whistle and gleefully proclaimed it was time to go "messing around." We threw down our spatulas and plungers and scrambled upstairs to change clothes. Mom exchanged her white socks and granny shoes for panty hose and red patent leather pumps. I cast off my grimy t-shirt, washed my armpits and donned a frilly dress. Looking fresh and perky in our frocks, we completed the ensemble with flowery hats and white gloves. Mom spritzed us with *Sois de Paris* toilet water (did it really come from a toilet?) She stuffed us into our *Monza Spider* convertible, stepped on the gas and sped toward downtown Dallas.

These special Saturday afternoons were tea parties in grand style. At *Titche's Tea Room*, gloved waitresses poured English breakfast tea from silver pitchers. *Wedgewood* china adorned the tables. Baskets bulged with tiny blueberry muffins, scones with clotted cream, and watercress sandwiches. A real live pianist played a *Steinway* grand piano as we sipped the warm beverage and raised our pinkies. Kathy and I used our inside voices, folded our napkins, and avoided food fights for at least an hour. Mommy was so proud.

Every sophisticated socialite spoke in hushed tones. If the whole experience wasn't glamorous enough, Elva the pianist pounded an arpeggiated flourish that signaled the start of the fashion show. Beautifully appointed models strode down the runway in rapid succession. They strutted their stuff as we gawked at the gorgeous duds. Suits from *Chanel,* scarves from *Hermes*, evening gowns from *Armani*, and bags from *Burberry* dazzled the onlookers. Mom would have to hock our convertible to buy an outfit. The models descended the stairs and visited each table, describing their ensembles and revealing their exorbitant prices. We pretended that the *Chanel* suit was a real bargain, but Mother knew all we could afford were the blueberry muffins.

Some Saturdays, I pretended I was swishing down the stairs like the stick-thin models, though my potato sack frame would look like a stuffed sausage in a strapless sheath. On rare occasions, a stately model would show off an A-line dress, which was "fashion speak" for "this will fit fatties." I dreamt a handsome prince would burst through the doors, slip a *Gucci* pump on my chubby appendage, and carry me away in his carriage.

Kathy, growing restless, was busy using the tablecloth for a napkin when her little linen square dropped to the floor. The strawberry jam on her cheeks added zip to the otherwise pristine white table runner. A snooty waitress sent a withering glance her way, but Kathy didn't care. She had paid for those muffins, by golly! (Or Mom did...) As the models disappeared back to the dressing room, Kathy seized the opportunity to do what she did best — to be the center of attention. She bounded up the stairs onto the runway, twirled three times, and showed the snooty ladies her jingle-bell petticoat. Instead of administering the whipping she deserved, Mommy giggled and applauded. The other ladies followed suit. Yep, tea parties were the best, for grown-up ladies and little girls alike. Only a loving, imaginative Mommy could watch her daughters sipping water from plastic teacups and fulfill their tea-party passion so completely. We left Titche's tearoom dazzled and delighted. Even our table manners improved...for the most part.

> *"The Lord your God is with you, He is mighty to save, He will take great delight in you, He will quiet you with His love, He will rejoice over you with singing."* (Zephaniah 3:17 NIV)

God's character is revealed in this passage in a highly personal, intimate way. How is He described? What is He doing?

What does this passage tell you about God as your Father? Personalize these words, and then pray a prayer of thanksgiving. "Thank you, God for always being with me, etc."

How does it make you feel that God is not just a cosmic Creator of the universe, but longs to be involved in every aspect of your life? Picture Him smiling at you through the day. See Him laughing when you are having fun, see Him singing over you as you worship Him.

Square Dancing:
We Need A Little Grace

G awky awkwardness can trip us up — in love and in life. Like porcupines, the closer we draw to others, the more deeply our prickles can wound them. We try to speak sensitively, but often we contract a bad case of "foot in mouth" disease. Only by God's help can we successfully navigate the choppy waters of family and friendship.

The Tacker girls (my sister, Kathy and I) were never fleet of foot. Mom spent her mad money attempting to morph her ugly ducklings into swans. We were subjected to "charm" lessons every Saturday morning without fail. Kathy and I paraded around the living room perimeter of Mrs. Nestor's house with phone books perched upon our heads. We were taught to simultaneously suck in our stomachs and smile without exploding. We learned to raise our pinkies when drinking tea. Alas, such feeble attempts to teach us poise and dignity were to no avail!

Mom's next stab at making us graceful was to enroll us in the *Happy Feet* dance studio. Day after day, we stumbled, pirouetted, bounced, and frequently fell on our behinds. It was not a pretty sight. But we were not alone. Most of the clumsy little ballerina wannabes in our class were similarly uncoordinated.

The worst part of dancing was the leotards — tight elastic dance-wear that made us look like little polish sausages. To add insult to injury, Mom had to buy us expensive "toe shoes." We were made to believe we could balance on our tippy toes for extended periods of time — excruciating *and* embarrassing!

My gym teacher at John W. Carpenter School, Coach Moe Hill, also tried to address the social awkwardness of his prepubescent pupils. Such nonsense was an exercise in futility! For example, Coach Hill initiated a Friday square dance class. I don't know what possessed him to think that eleven-year-old boys and girls would forget that the opposite sex had "cooties." The balding, jolly gentleman hoped he'd magically convince his pupils to peacefully coexist. Square dance music was especially annoying. Even at my tender age of eleven, a foray into redneck Country and Western tunes offended my classical music sensibilities.

Sixth grade boys were no prize, I can assure you. They seldom bathed or brushed their teeth, they frequently smelled like sweat, and they spent most of their waking hours burping the alphabet or trying to make farting sounds with their armpits. Sixth grade girls were no better. Most of us wore glasses and braces, sprouted our first pimples, and hadn't shed our baby fat. (I'm still waiting for that to happen). Friday gym classes only escalated our mutual loathing. Couldn't we just relieve our pent-up hostility by lobbing dodge balls at each other? But Coach Hill never wavered. Friday would, amid great protest, still remain square dance day. He played the same four twangy songs on his squeaky record player: *"Honey, Don't Come Home Drinking with Loving on Your Mind," "Ring of Fire," "Buffalo Gal, Won't You Come Out Tonight?"* and *"Turkey in the Straw."* The coach cheerily cranked up the volume to an ear-splitting level, donned his straw hat, and proceeded to assume the role of "square dance caller." He barked complex dance steps like "promenade," "allemande left" and "swing your partner."

Our classmates attempted to follow the caller's directions, but as soon as we clasped clammy palms with a creepy partner, things started to get ugly. By the first *do-si-do*, we muttered mean names at each other under our breaths. Soon we squeezed each others' hands so hard our cereal-box mood rings turned purple. Hand-squeezing escalated to foot-stomping, and foot-stomping always led to chaos. One cloudy Friday morning in particular, the natives were restless. Our squares kept morphing into trapezoids and parallelograms. Coach Hill was also on edge — probably because it was "fish stick Friday" and he could not stomach the idea of downing a lukewarm lump of breaded fish guts. Our class was scheduled just before lunch.

Coach called us to attention with his silver whistle and the ancient tribal ritual ensued. My partner, Steve Parish, was a freckle-faced, tow-headed boy with hair the texture of a Brillo pad and feet the size of swim fins. As soon as we started our promenade, Steve stomped on my right foot. I naturally assumed this was a random act of klutziness. But then the foot-pulverizing became harder and more deliberate. I quivered at every *allemande right*. I could feel tears welling up, and I limped over to the bleachers at the side of the gym. My toes were already turning a sickly shade of purple. The coach witnessed the atrocity and quickly banished Steve Parish to Principal Moffett's office.

I racked my brain, wondering why Steve had been so cruel. Why was I the object of his hostility and pent-up aggression? I didn't know the answer until after lunch. Coach Hill summoned me to his little glass office. His lips were quivering as he seemed to hold back a giggle. "You see, Julie," he snickered, "this young man has a crush on you — and the only way he knows to express his adoration is to tease you by obliterating your arches. It won't happen again." I was stunned. This assault was Steve's attempt at romance?

Coach shuffled the squares the next week, and Steve never looked me in the eye again. I was stuck with Melvin McElroy and he didn't care if I lived or died. When I sneaked a peek at Steve, something within me softened. I realized how easily we can hurt the ones we love. We may not be foot-stompers, but too often we wound the ones we care about the most. The closer we get, the more easily we can cause each other pain. Many summer afternoons, I pedaled my

Schwinn bike up the alley and looked longingly at Steve's bedroom window. Unrequited love is so bittersweet.

I later learned Steve became a wealthy podiatrist — a foot doctor. Go figure!

Relationships are often rocky. We live in an imperfect world. We are imperfect people. So, be assured, we will hurt each other. The key is to humble ourselves and keep on loving. Live with grace, patience and forgiveness.

> *"Be completely humble and gentle; be patient, bearing with one another in love. Make every effort to keep the unity of the Spirit through the bond of peace."* (Ephesians 4:2-4)

Paul teaches several key principles about relating to others in these verses. List all the words that the apostle uses to describe what loving someone looks like. List the adjectives, one after the other. Is there a progression? Do we need to be humble, patient, and gentle to bear the "prickles" of others?

What are some ways you can be a peacemaker at home or at work? Do you make it your passion to heal conflict and strife in relationships? Who is the source of unity, according to these verses? How are unity and peace related?

Think of someone you know who is difficult to love. Using the encouragement above, write them a card, say a kind word, text them, or call them on the phone. Let them know you value their friendship.

What are some ways you can be a peacemaker at home or at work? Do you make it your passion to heal conflict and strife in relationships?

iMath:
At Least God Knows How to Count

My daughter, Bronwyn, is a full-fledged software-toting, binary-coding computer geek. She can memorize endless strings of numbers and algorhythms. I have trouble remembering what I had for lunch. Bronwyn did have a head start on the math genes, however. Three of her four grandparents were accountants and generously donated their number prowess to my youngest young'un. I do have a weird knack of memorizing random phone numbers of people I never intend to call. My *iPhone* keeps track of all my finances, but I never trust its little nano chip security system. Even now, some Mac genius is probably hacking into my checking account to purchase the latest version of *Guitar Hero*.

How could I totally miss an aptitude for all things numerical? I hate prime numbers. I love prime rib. I carried my ones, but forgot where I put them. Decimals decimate me and fractions fracture my fragile ego. The only *pi* I eye is the pecan pastry I slather with whipped cream after supper. How could this apple fall so far from the family tree?

My parents tried to teach me number-crunching as a youngster. Mom started with "this little piggy went to the market," and tried subtracting roast beef from the "little piggy that had none," but I always ran out of toes. Besides, talking about roast beef made me want to quit counting and start chewing. I thought it rather barbaric that little Porky the Pig chowed down on his barnyard buddy, Bossy the Cow. Who made up that nursery rhyme, anyway?

Daddy had an old-timey calculator that was my toy as a toddler. *The Count* on *Sesame Street* had not yet appeared on the *PBS* lineup, so Daddy tried to entertain me with his accounting machine from work. I pressed the number keys, turned the crank, and little digits appeared at the top bar like cherries on a slot machine. I used the calculator to play the number pads like piano keys. I didn't care about finding answers, but I did get the urge to play the slots in Vegas.

Mommy recognized my failure at figures, so she stacked cans of peas, beets, and corn from the pantry and asked me to count each one. She then coached me to determine how many aluminum cylinders remained when she removed them. We always ended up in a food fight, throwing cans will-nilly. I loved playing vegetable roulette, but I hid the peach and pudding cans in case things got ugly.

Dad bought me an abacus for my fourth birthday. An abacus is a toy that Chinese parents use to teach their tots how to add and subtract. The toy had red wooden balls suspended on wires so a child could move them back and forth to *add* or *take away*. Kathy thought the red balls were cherries, so my abacus ended up in her *"stomacus."* Fortunately, wood is a great source of fiber and we retrieved the balls, smelly but unscathed, the next morning.

My parents were hopeful the school system would provide my much-needed calculation education. Mrs. Chase, the first grade Bunny class teacher, wrote addition problems on the blackboard. She handed a piece of chalk to each child and instructed them to scrawl the total in front of God and everybody. Every kid scribbled their answer and quickly scrambled back to their seat. I alone remained standing, clueless and humiliated. George, my first-grade flame, saw my dilemma and hurled an eraser at the back of Mrs. Chase's head. As she scoured the room for the culprit, George saved my bacon by hurriedly completing the cipher on my behalf. I felt so loved — like Cinderella being rescued by Prince Charming from the evil dragon teacher.

My math finally improved when I moved on to second grade. Mrs. Olson, my second grade teacher, was the undisputed coolest teacher in L.O. Donald elementary school. Wispy-thin with a winning smile, Avis Olson was a joy to watch. I listened to her soothing voice even through addition and subtraction. This was no ordinary feat because her competition was dreamy Gary Wallace, who sat in front of me. He wore his navy blue Cub Scout suit on Wednesdays, and I could never resist a man in uniform. Gary greased his flat top with Vitalis pomade, and the smell wafted sensuously toward my desk.

But even Gary Wallis could not rival Mrs. Olson's creative antics. On Monday mornings, life-sized cardboard cutouts of the Campbell's Soup Kids came out of the closet near her desk. Each Kid held a specific number, and we added and subtracted Campbell's Kids until recess. Later on, when she tried to teach us how to "carry our ones," she hauled out Aunt Jemima to help.

My major integer dilemma came when Mrs. Pheobe Carvil, my third grade math teacher, had a nervous breakdown in October. (I hope I didn't give it to her.) The frizzy-haired sub, Mr. Dripple, knew less about math than I did. Dripple sat at his desk, picked his toes, and gave us the run of the classroom. We giggled, played tag, chucked erasers, and scraped the desk undersides for leftover *Double Bubble* chewing gum. We learned absolutely nothing about multiplication or long division, and spent the remainder of the semester in blissful ignorance. (This is the absolute truth.)

My come-uppance came during the *Iowa Tests*. These standardized brain-teasers were designed to pigeonhole people into brainiac and moron classifications. My scores were always the same — 99% on the verbal portion, .0006 on the math portion. My teachers were in a quandary. I was too smart to be held back and too dumb in math to promote. Finally, they realized I was so high maintenance, no teacher wanted to have me more than once.

By middle school, I developed some rather clever coping mechanisms for my math deficiencies. I asked the teacher so many dumb questions during class that she forgot to give us homework, and I learned how to fake my own death on quiz days. Geometry was particularly challenging because my classmates were so competitive. Nerdy Roy Ferguson, dressed like "James Bond," etched his geometry homework on glass, and delivered it with *Mission Impossible* playing in the background. Who can top that? Prissy Nancy Neal, not to be outdone by Roy's creativity, baked a fudge sheet cake and drew the answers with white icing. Nancy's homework didn't last. We couldn't wait to test her next trapezoid and isosceles triangles. Miss George's class had its fun moments, but when geometry class concluded, I was always on a tangent. *(Pardon the math pun.)*

High school math avoidance was much easier. I took so many electives, I didn't have room for anything in my schedule but algebra and trig. I cuddled up to Jeff, the trigonometry savant, and went steady with him until the semester was over. Then I dumped him for Marshall Millsap, the algebra nerd. He tutored me late at night and I traded him smooches for answers. I have since repented in dust and ashes. I do believe I spurred my math tutors to greatness. Dr. Jeff (Toothy) Ferguson became an orthodontist. He counts molars and bicuspids all day and charges an arm and a leg for it. Dorky Marshall is global vice-president of Chase Bank and is happily counting his money in Tahiti.

As for me, I majored in music in college. Musicians only have to count to four.

> *"Blessed are those whose transgressions are forgiven, whose sins are covered. Blessed is the one whose sin the Lord will never count against them. Is this blessedness only for the circumcised, or also for the uncircumcised? We have been saying that Abraham's faith was credited to him as righteousness."* (Romans 4:7-9 NIV)

Is God good at math? He counts every sparrow (Matthew 10:29). He counts His sheep and has not lost a single one (John 10:14-18). But there are things that He chooses not to count. When we invite Jesus Christ into our lives and trust that His death on the cross paid the debt for our sins, He refuses to count. Notice the word that precedes "count" in verse eight. In your heart of hearts, do you truly believe that you are forgiven by God, that your debt of sin is paid in full? List some of your sins here. Now write "paid in full" over the list.

In verse nine, Paul writes that Abraham's faith was credited to him as righteousness. "Credited" is an accounting term. It means that he was right with God because God saw his faith "deposit" and verified that it was valid. Picture your life as a

bank. Imagine God pouring His riches into your account. How does that make you feel?

Remember a time when someone forgave you. Who were they? Remember a time when you forgave someone else for a wrong they had done to you. What was it? Are you still holding onto the grudge, or have you cancelled the debt? Spend some moments praying for God to give you a forgiving heart, even as He has forgiven you.

Me First

School lunch lines were hazardous to my health.

"**O**kay kids, no pinching, poking, pushing, kicking, tripping or tickling," warned Mrs. Chase, my first grade teacher. Six-year-old boys can be incredibly inventive. My teacher failed to outlaw toe-crushing, elbowing, "wet-willying," ponytail tugging, or snot-spraying. With such an arsenal of lunch line weaponry, no defenseless girl was safe from the "cafeteria beasts" that surrounded her. Day after day, the drill was the same—and all for what? Some stringy green beans, half-cooked macaroni, and a lukewarm box of milk? I was no idiot. After the third day of school, I brought my sack lunch from home, even if I had to make it myself. I shoved whatever green or brown goo I could find in the *Frigidaire* into my *Tupperware* box and loaded up on vanilla wafers.

Lunch line torture was not my first experience with standing in line. Oddly enough, I loved standing in the grocery line with

Mommy in my toddler days. If the checker took too long at the *A & P*, Mommy pulled me out of my baby seat and let me rest my head on her soft-sweatered shoulder. I dozed off sniffing the aroma of baked chicken, *Pine Sol*, and apple pie. Grocery checkout lines became more exciting as I grew older. While Mother lamented over the price of ground beef, I scarfed two *Twizzlers*, three *Milky Ways*, and a *Peppermint Patty* right under her nose. No one noticed except the obnoxious little tattletale in the cart behind me. I lived a miserable, candy-less life for a week.

By the age of eleven, I was tall enough to reach the teen magazines in the *Safeway* grocery line. Did Donny Osmond have his teeth capped? I had to know! Did the Beatles really have a yellow submarine? Would Mom let me have a polka-dot miniskirt like Twiggy, even if I looked like Miss Piggy? I didn't care how long it took to buy *Wheaties*. I was transported to teen paradise. Now the only thing I learn from standing next to the grocery line magazines is if Britney Spears remembered to take her bipolar medication.

My grocery store line experiences have changed in the past few years. I'm always in a hurry. Can I get away with standing in the fifteen-item express line if I have two items of the same thing? What if I hide the grape jelly underneath my purse? Is the bag boy like the grocery police, counting every cereal box and veggie can to see if I've gone over my limit? Will I be arrested for express line fraud, handcuffed and banished to the back of the store by the toilet paper? Will my face appear on the Kroger "most wanted" list? I couldn't help myself. I had to push the envelope. After multiple infractions, I have repented of "line fraud." I now grocery shop at *Walmart* between 2:00 and 4:00 a.m. No waiting on aisle five.

Amusement parks are supposed to be fun. But in reality, *Disney, Dollywood, Six Flags over Somewhere*, and *Mr. Knott* have persuaded gullible parents everywhere to spend exorbitant amounts of money for the privilege of standing in line. Think about it. How many rides do kids actually get to ride on a hot twelve-hour June day? Seven? Eight? I'm guessing most folks are paying forty bucks a pop to wait, wait some more, get nauseated, get wet, get scared, and get off a sixty-second ride.

Disney designers try to hoodwink their visitors by decorating rows and rows of rope to resemble the ride ahead. Don't be fooled. It's really wheat paste, spray paint, and a little plastic ivy. It's hot, humid, and dark and has nothing to do with fun. A decade ago, some clever media mogul decided to install TV monitors to watch while waiting in "ride lines." The amusement wizards didn't play one of the gazillion *Star Wars* movies or *Pixar* cartoons (after all, I *will* be standing in that same spot for a good hour and a half). Instead, these gurus have a camera trained on the poor schmucks who get to ride the ride before I do. By the time it's my turn to whirl in the teacups or hurl on *Space Mountain*, the whole experience is old hat.

Line "bandits" should go to prison. I saw one kid at *Six Flags* pull up to the front of every ride in a wheelchair, then at closing time he removed his plastic cast and ran to his car. Line "cutters" really chap my hide. One time I was minding my own business in the security line at the airport when an attractive blonde pretended she recognized a homely salesman some twenty people ahead of her. He was so flattered and startled, he stepped aside and let her stand in front of him. That hussy, that self-absorbed "line-schlepper," flopped her *Gucci* bag on the x-ray belt, flitted by the security guy, and gave the peons behind her a knowing wink. I should have slipped some C-4 in her bag as she swished by.

"Line savers" are just as devious. I was innocently standing in line at Starbucks, waiting to order my grande soy double caramel mocha *frappucino* no-whip (extra hot) when the man in front of me stepped aside to make room for his large wife and seven children, none of whom had any idea what they wanted to order. I finished reading Tolstoy's *War and Peace* while little Sadie tried to decide if she wanted the pumpkin muffin or the cheesecake brownie. By now, everyone behind me had left the store to get in the drive-thru line.

U.S. government employees have turned waiting in line into trauma and torture. You might as well go to Gitmo. On my last visit, I entered the D. M. V. building. It always smells like feet. There were hundreds of lines, and I couldn't tell where any of them went. As I scoped out the gigantic room the size of *Costco*, I noticed hundreds of unmarked booths with unidentified employees looking both angry and disinterested at the same time. How do I get to see these people, and why do I want to? Finally, I wandered toward some frizzy-haired lady with horn-rimmed glasses, and she mumbled that I should take a number. I was herded like an innocent sheep to slaughter toward a room with one door and no windows. There was no escape.

Soon I discovered that six other people in line had the same number as I did. The frizzy-haired lady failed to tell me that I needed a "letter" as well. So I went back to where I started. The truck driver behind me had B. O. and a nasty head cold, but I'm a Christian, so I waited patiently. At long last, my number flashed "B-5" and I raced over to the rickety chair awaiting my grateful behind. At long last, a skinny man in a leisure suit asked me to follow him to a parking lot filled with orange cones. "You have two tries to parallel-park," he droned. "But I came to change my car title!" I gasped. So I got my mug photo snapped for a new driver's license (that I didn't need). I knew I should have brushed my teeth! I limped out of the building, and my Ford was still registered in Texas instead of Arizona. Now I take the bus.

In England, lines are called *queues*, a name that seems much more civil and refined for standing in line with one's fellow man. Perhaps the English actually use words like "pardon me" or "after you." We could learn a thing or two from our genteel neighbors across the pond. Jesus said that "the last shall be first and the first shall be last." Courtesy is an oft-ignored Christian virtue.

Maybe there will be no lines in heaven. Perhaps we'll all stand in clumps and huddle up!

But the fruit of the Spirit is love, joy, peace, patience, kindness, goodness, faithfulness, gentleness and self-control. Against such things there is no law. Those who belong to Christ Jesus have crucified the sinful nature with its passions and desires. Since we live by the Spirit, let us keep in step with the Spirit. Let us not become conceited, provoking and envying each other. (Galatians 5:22–26 NIV)

The "fruits" of the Holy Spirit are also the character traits of Jesus Christ. When you are filled with Christ, you resemble Him in every way. Which "fruits" do you lack in your life?

Consider the fruits of the Spirit that show up in your life. For example, what does kindness look like in your everyday life? Do you show deference and courtesy to others? Do you say "please" and "thank you"? Do you wait patiently for others who are older or slower than you? Do you wait upon others as Jesus would? List some ways you could be more kind and courteous.

Now, list some people around you who need to receive more attention and courtesy. Choose one, and take a moment to call or e-mail that person with a word of encouragement.

Beauford
It's Really Hard to Wait and Come

D r. Woof, our vet, assures me that most canines have the emotional and intellectual capacity of a two-year-old. I disagree. Toddlers are much dumber than doggies, and I have hard evidence to prove it. The average toddler spews his strained spinach all over Mom's white blouse and tosses his cookies against the kitchen cabinet. Most doggies have the good sense to bolt anything down, edible or not. Nary a crumb is wasted.

When our puppy, Beauford, my sister's mini-doxie, was just a baby wiener dog, Kathy dressed him in a fireman's suit (helmet, ax and all) and dragged him to a kiddie Halloween party. The poor pup was slapped around, tail-pulled, and slobbered on by the neighborhood preschoolers. Beauford was mildly annoyed, but was clever as a fox. So he made like a fire dog, lifted his leg and squirted from his "fire hydrant" at any oncoming kiddie. Finally, Bo-Bo, the red-suited wiener, was free to roam around the grassy playground, scarfing leftover gummy bears and taffy from the kiddies' goody bags. When my sis Kathy, Beauford's pet human, had her back turned, Bo-Bo concocted his evil plan. Kathy was inhaling a blob of cotton candy when she heard a loud "snarfing" noise in the direction of our devious dog. He was looking rather "green around the gills," so Sissy picked her baby up to see what was the matter. A putrid fleshy orb protruded from his tiny piehole, causing him to choke and gasp for breath. In one quick yank, Kathy extracted a king-size foot-long *Oscar Meyer* wiener from her pint-sized pooch. The half-masticated sausage was almost as big as his entire body. Bo-Bo collapsed on the pavement and gave Sis a grateful tail wag and sigh, all the while thinking of how he could get that lunch meat down his gullet again. Most toddlers can't manage to be that swift and sneaky before the age of three. Really.

Beauford, like most celebrity rat dogs, had his own unique sense of style. His favorite duds were his *Dallas Cowboys* sweatshirt for chilly mornings, his Sunday best pink Polo button-down, his striped Nike golf shirt for a sporty look, and his Christmas pajamas replete with jingle bells and blinking lights. He did, however, make one fashion *faux paw* when he allowed us to dress him like a hotdog for the Sunday afternoon picnic. Nobody saw it coming. A Doberman named Aldo took one look at the pickles, onions, mustard, ketchup, and special sauce on Bo-Bo's hot dog duds and decided Beauford looked too delectable to resist. If Daddy had not intervened, poor

Bo-Bo would have been Aldo's tasty lunch. No more "food-themed" costumes for him!

I saw Beauford naked one day and had to avert my eyes. He was equally mortified and dashed behind our fish tank to hide his shame. Two-year-olds consider clothing to be optional. In fact, they spend most of their energy running away from any adult attempting to clothe them. Once attired, the little nippers take the most inopportune moments to disrobe — usually in a December snowstorm or in front of snooty Aunt Bulimia on Thanksgiving.

My sister Kathy, in her terrible twos, was not nearly as modest as our fuzzy black and tan pup. At the tender age of two-and-a-half, Kathy scaled the carpeted stairs leading to our church pulpit with her shiny pink hiney glistening for the entire congregation to see. Bess Milam, the Women's Missionary Union president, screamed, "Demon baby, demon baby!" and passed out in a heap on Clinton Feemster, the head usher. Pop rushed from his pew to hide her nakedness, but the church at large had already concluded that the Tacker family tolerated nudity and had liberal Unitarian leanings.

Unlike modest, fashion-conscious, metrosexual Beauford, two-year-old Kathy had the annoying habit of removing her underwear any time it chafed or felt itchy. Mom was always the last person to learn of her shenanigans, so to save face as a good deacon's wife, she sewed suspenders on Sissy's droopy drawers and prayed Kathy would not become a stripper when she turned twenty-one.

Beauford was also much more worldly-wise than his kiddie counterparts. He took one look at the neighbor's gorgeous red-headed retriever, Shelby, and fell madly in love. Being a "dog of the world," he was "twitterpated" and determined to make Shelby his bride. The only obstacle to their fiery passion was that furry Shelby was three times Beauford's size, and the only thing small enough for Bo-Bo to hump was Shelby's face. Shelby got the message anyway and they went steady for years. Although he had a wandering eye for the occasional sexy Shitzu or perky poodle, Beauford never forgot his first love.

Most overgrown twosie babies spend half of their time slamming into coffee tables, tripping over Daddy's shoes, and running into walls. Our doxie was much too wily and lazy for that. He convinced us that he must be carried from place to place with two or more blankets and chew-toys in tow. To avoid leaping, scampering, slipping, or limping like most pooches, Beauford simply whined until Kathy and I built carpeted ramps leading up to our king-sized bed and favorite recliner. He "prissily" pranced from place to place with elegance and style. No toddler has enough moxie to pull that off.

Potty-training is a challenge "twofers" seldom conquer until the age of three, and in the case of boys, until high school. Buzzer bells, *Gummy Bears* and potty chairs seldom coax the little buggers to do their business. Why can't they figure out what the big ivory bowl is for? Beauford knew. It was a cooling drinking fountain on a warm day and a Jacuzzi when he was feeling a little *verklempt*. Yes, the prissy little pooch knew he was supposed to go outside to poop, but if the weather was cold or rainy, he simply backed up to the dog door and stuck his booty just far enough through the hole to leave his little brown present. After all, he didn't want to get his *Cowboys'* sweater wet.

I haven't even mentioned Beauford's sister, Bailey. His fuzzy bearded sister was a bit of a whiner. She was nervous, "barky," and afraid of her own shadow. But poor Beej lived with Beauford. Of course, she needed the dog whisperer. She never knew if her dinner would magically disappear from her bowl. She tried to guard the backyard from bunnies, bugs, and burglars, but Bo-Bo was no help at all. He remained happily ensconced on his leather recliner, whiling away the hours watching "Animal Planet." No wonder Bailey was on Valium. Toddlers are much less frustrating than Beauford. He turned emotional abuse into an art form.

Yes, Bo-Bo was almost human – checking himself out when he sauntered by a mirror. He would not rest his posterior until a fresh, warm, fluffy blankie was pulled out of the dryer for him. Beau barked at the dogs on the television and criticized their hack method acting with a snarl and a sneer. He ate when he wanted, where he wanted, and demanded the finest cuisine. No plain kibble for him! Beauford was certainly sharper than his blubbery two-year-old counterparts. He had trained his humans well, by golly. Maybe we should have been the trainers instead of the trainees!

Dog trainers know the secret of God's purpose. No matter what distractions the master-trainer places around the pet — a juicy t-bone, a petulant cat, a supersonic ear-splitting pitch — the well-trained canine never loses eye-contact with his master. In a calm voice, the master says, "Wait....wait....come!" And the doggie comes. Every time. We must learn to do the same. Suffering's divine purpose is to fix our eyes on our Master without wavering. Grief and loss wound us. "Wait." A trusted friend betrays us. "Wait." Financial reversals shake us. "Wait." And "wait" is always followed by, "Come." God wants us to fix our eyes on Him. Take our cues from Him. Surrender to His wise wishes for our lives.

So wait. Wait. Waaaaait. Come!

To Thee I lift up my eyes,
O Thou who art enthroned in the heavens!
2 Behold, as the eyes of servants look to the hand of their
master,
As the eyes of a maid to the hand of her mistress;
So our eyes look to the LORD our God,
Until He shall be gracious to us. (Psalm 123:1-2 NASB)

How do we keep our eyes focused upon God? What would that look like? According to verse one, why should we look to Him?

These verses describe God's position and authority. Describe Him in your own words. Write a message of adoration and praise to Him.

The maid in verse two looked carefully to follow her mistress's cues. Are you in tune with the cues for daily living that God is giving you? The psalmist encourages us to persistently "look to the LORD our God." What is the result? How has waiting upon God and depending upon Him changed your life? Pray and ask God to make you more sensitive to His leading today.

Prince Charming:
My Love Story With Jesus

Books were my friends when I was a wee one. My parents owned countless black-and-white snapshots of me snoring, sprawled on top of my flowered bedspread, covered in fairy tales and animal adventures. I traveled to faraway places or made a secret rendezvous with the prince of my dreams with just the flip of a page. My treasured tomes came in all shapes and sizes. The flimsy cardboard models came from the grocery store. Mom purchased the page-turners in desperation when I went ballistic in the candy aisle. She let me use my wax crayons on the cheapie cardboard books like *Pokey Little Puppy*. I drew in extra characters and added trees and flowers with magenta and yellow-orange. Hardback books were much more precious. Mom placed them out of reach on a high wooden shelf next to *Peter Rabbit*. These treasured books only came down to visit at bedtime when Daddy read to me. I touched their slick painted pages in awe and wonder. Occasionally, after bedtime,

I pulled my rocking chair up to the bookshelf to sneak a peek. The living room coffee table housed enormous decorative books—glorious and too heavy to lift. Daddy loved art museums, so the family often gathered on the sofa after supper to gawk at the masterpieces of Renoir, Monet, Rembrandt and Van Gogh.

I learned many valuable lessons from my storybooks. If the *Little Engine that Could* had dutifully tugged his caboose up the mountain twice a day and laid off the chips and banana splits back at the station, he would have "thought he could" much earlier in the tale. *Red Riding Hood* was asking for trouble when she wore that racy red outfit. If she had donned the simple gingham frock that her mother had laid out for her, the lusty Big Bad Wolf would have overlooked her and devoured a nearby bunny instead. The air-headed *Three Little Pigs* were morons. If they had hired out their construction job to the responsible woodsman from Red Riding Hood's neighborhood, the Big Bad Wolf would have ceased his incessant huffing and puffing. The windbag would have given up his penchant for barbecued pork to become a vegetarian. Besides, no wolf topples a house, no matter how hard he blows. With hot air like that, Wolfie could have pursued a career as a preacher or a politician. Either way, he could earn a boatload of pork bellies without nabbing the three little swine. Goldilocks should have been jailed for breaking and entering the *Three Bears'* happy home. I imagined her high-maintenance stint in the pokey aggravating the prison guards, as she whined about her cot being "too hard or too soft" instead of "just right." Lock her in the slammer for good. She should have known better! Foolish characters! There was not a role model among them!

Grandpa Boy's yarns were wonderfully captivating. His imaginary villains were named *Gee-Whizicuss, Wallygopper, Boogiesnarf and Halitosis.* The monstrous creatures lurked in the backyard shadows on moonless nights. Only our muscle-bound Grandfather and his imaginary sidekick, Johnny Squirrel, could easily outsmart them. As I listened to Boy's adventures (sound effects and all), I traveled the globe with him and Johnny to exotic destinations in search of pretend enemies. My pulse raced, my heart pounded and my eyes grew round as saucers. When Grandpa and I returned from battle safe and sound, I drifted off on Grandpa's cuddly shoulder, feeling safe and cozy. Johnny Squirrel, scampering in the pecan tree above the bedroom window, always emerged victorious. *"Bond. James Bond,"* was not coined by Ian Fleming. Fleming stole it from Grandpa Boy. Our wooly hero triumphantly trounced his foes, and when onlookers asked his name, he slyly replied, *"Squirrel. Johnny Squirrel."*

Comic books were a cheap read and only led to trouble. The cartoon tales only cost a nickel but they did a lot of damage to my psyche. *Dennis the Menace* taught me much about mischief. If I hadn't learned to infuriate my parents before, Dennis gave me all the ammo I needed. *Richie Rich*, the spoiled tycoon's son, taught his readers the importance of money-grubbing materialism. All of a sudden, my ten-cent allowance seemed like a pittance. Olive Oil, the sweetheart of *Popeye* the sailor man, was an anorexic whiner. Poor Popeye exercised regularly and ate his spinach, but still couldn't please her. I learned the fine art of whining from Olive. The super-hero comics fascinated me, too. *Superman, Batman, Spiderman* and *Wonder Woman* always trounced evil geniuses like the *Joker* and *Lex Luthor*. But superheroes were just that. Their powers were unattainable, leaving their young readers feeling ordinary and inadequate. Save your comic book nickel and spend it on a Popsicle.

Love stories always held a mysterious fascination for me. *Cinderella's* Prince Charming had a shoe fetish and found his true love barefoot and in need of a pair of *Jimmy Choos*. Good Sunday shoes are hard to find, and princes are in even shorter supply. Some women would rather have glamorous footwear than a ne'er-do-well prince any day. The nameless prince in *Snow White* could have been an idiot for all we know. He hopped on his horse and followed his nose to Sleepy, Dopey and Grumpy's cottage. Alas! His true love snored like a train, frozen in a cryogenic coma. Snow White's sweetheart had only one redeeming quality — he delivered a kiss that could wake the dead. Prince Hot Lips shoved his tongue down Snow White's throat and roused her from her cold sleep. One would hope that after the clueless fellow realized the vain, wicked queen's chicanery, he'd send his nasty mom to rehab or put her behind bars. That lady had serious anger issues. Now *Sleeping Beauty's* prince was a guy with real backbone. He scaled thorny castle walls and valiantly parried with a giant dragon-lady who looked amazingly like *Cruella DeVille* from *101 Dalmatians*. The Walt Disney animators had no imagination. One villainess looked like another. *The Frog Prince* was my favorite romantic tale. The warty amphibian morphed into a prince only after a hot babe smooched him on the lips. Most boys I knew looked a lot more like frogs than princes.

Although all stories held some fascination for me, only one special storybook changed my life. *More Little Visits with God* was prominently perched on the shelf above my headboard. Mom read *Little Visits* to me every night. In fact, I still own it to this day. One chilly Saturday morning, I crouched on the laundry room floor with my back to the dryer. The air vents were warm and comforted my frosty toes. I gazed for a long time at a picture of Jesus holding little children in His lap. He was smiling and hugging them gently. The happy kids had red, yellow, black and white faces. Some were pudgy, some were skinny. Some had freckles, others had slanted eyes. A few children were well-dressed and others were in rags. In that hushed moment, I heard Jesus speak to me as clearly as if He had sat down with His arm around me in that cozy laundry room. "Julie," He said, "come up here. Sit on my lap. I will hold you close to me always. I will love you and take care of you." In my heart of hearts, I trusted that this quiet voice was real and this moment was monumental. As a four-year-old girl, I didn't comprehend redemption, sanctification, or substitutionary atonement. I just knew that Jesus knew me and loved me.

Before big church and before kindergarten, I met the real Jesus. I felt His warm love and I was certain He would keep His promise. That was the beginning of my story. I know a happy ending awaits. And the rest—well, it's a real page-turner.

> *"Jesus said to them, "Let the little children come to me, and do not hinder them, for the kingdom of God belongs to such as these."* (Mark 10:13-16 NIV)

Jesus taught his disciples many in His encounter with these little children. What are some of the principles taught in this passage? Write them here.

How does Jesus' response to the children make you feel? Is this your view of Jesus, or do you see Him as more impersonal and rejecting? Take time to memorize the above verse and meditate on it this week.

List some of your earliest encounters with Jesus. Spend some time thanking the God who wants to hold you and be your constant companion, comforter, and protector. If you have not received Jesus' free gift of salvation, pray and ask Him to come into your life. He will love you, never leave you, and keep you close to His heart.

The Get-Well Box

My fifth year of life was a nightmare. *Captain Kangaroo* had lost Green Jeans. No, that's not what the Captain wore; Green Jeans was his hilarious sidekick who made my favorite kiddie TV show worth watching. KTVT, our local public television station, tried to dam the flood of plummeting ratings by compensating with a local yokel named *Mr. Peppermint*. Every kid knew Peppermint was a sorry substitute for Green Jeans. Mickey and Amanda Mud Turtle, Mr. Peppermint's lame puppets, taught bored five-year-olds the alphabet. Why would we want to learn our ABC's on TV? Wasn't that the sole purpose of kindergarten?

Unfortunately, the television would soon become my sole source of companionship. My two-year-old sister, Kathy, was worthless in the friend department. All she knew how to do was cry and break all my toys. My babysitter, Mrs. Richardson, was nice enough. But she only made lunch and put us in time-out when we sassed her or trashed the living room.

I had high hopes for kindergarten. Mrs. Drake's *School for Eager Beavers* was a white wooden-framed house on the end of our cul-de-sac. The idyllic little home displayed a school-bell sign on the front lawn. As a four-year-old, I spent lazy afternoons under our mimosa tree, watching happy youngsters spilling out of her front door, squealing with delight. Yes, Mrs. Drake's *School for Eager Beavers* was akin to paradise in my estimation—a veritable wonderland escape from the monotony of home life.

I crossed off the sultry summer days on our refrigerator calendar. As the grasshopper chirps subsided and chiggers ceased to chomp, the brisk fall air signaled my chance at freedom. I obtained the required list of school supplies from the *Rexall* on the corner: a box of pencils, a 24-pack of *Crayolas*, a lined tablet, and a *Yosemite Sam* lunchbox with matching thermos. The list was scanty, but Eager Beavers were just beginning scholastic endeavors that would dominate the next thirteen years of life. Five-year-olds have the energy of a bunny and the attention span of a gnat.

The greatest challenge of kindergarten was naptime. We weren't allowed to talk, wiggle, or poke our neighbors. If you blatantly disregarded the "nap code," you could say goodbye to mid-afternoon *Oreos* and milk. I learned later that naptime was not designed for us to catch up on our sleep. It was for Mrs. Drake to catch up on her sanity.

September blew by quickly. I was getting my kindergarten sea legs: only one girl was at the top of the pecking order, burps and booger-picking were taboo, and nobody—yes, nobody, was allowed to make jokes about Tommy Tugbottom's last name. He was feisty and packed a punch. In retrospect, I realized that poor boy would go through life fighting a battle, just like the surly Texas governor, Jim Hogg, who named his girls Ima and Eura. Sadist!

October rolled around, and I was a kindergarten pro. I knew my ABC's, I could count to a thousand without blinking an eye, and I learned to dunk my *Oreos* in my milk while Mrs. Drake picked up the blocks or snored in her seat after story time. After all, twenty five-year-olds could squeeze the life out of any self-respecting grownup.

Then disaster struck. Just as we started tracing Halloween pump-kins and the fall air turned chill, I got sick. My temperature soared, and my head hurt. Mom rushed me to the doctor's office. Dr. Pharaoh was my debonair pediatrician. No, he was not Egyptian royalty, but he was pretty cool. The good doctor had dark, wavy hair, a toothy grin, and a starched white coat that stood up by itself.

Although Dr. Pharaoh's office was chock-full of blocks, choo-choo trains, and *Highlights* magazines, every kid knew the brutal truth: behind those brightly colored doors lurked a nurse with a shot. An unwitting toddler would lumber through the *Magic Kingdom* entrance, and moments later the waiting room rocked with blood-curdling shrieks. Adults think shots are innocuous little pinpricks, but children know the truth. They are evil, giant metal cylinders designed to inflict terror in their hearts and torture to their pink pudgy posteriors. I didn't know why grown-ups got to roll up their sleeves and receive dignified little pinpricks. As a child, the drill was always the same. Bend over, moon the nurse, and get mercilessly stabbed by a gloating grown-up.

Dr. Pharaoh swaggered into the examining room as I sat perched on a freezing, tissue-covered table in my underwear or a tiny hospital gown with the open back blowing in the breeze. I believe it is part of the art of physician-intimidation. He grinned as if I would be excited to see him. "How's my little trooper today?" he queried. Before I could answer, he gagged me with a tongue depressor and poked me vigorously in the tummy. "A few too many vanilla wafers, huh?" the doc smirked. I was full of *Reese's Pieces*, and it was none of his business! "Let's look in those little ears . . . " He poked and prodded. "Wow, you could grow flowers in that earwax." I was incensed. Mom tried to stick soapy Q-tips in my ear holes occasionally, but to no avail. Ear hygiene felt like receiving a wet willy. I reasoned that my mousy brown locks covered my ears anyway.

After the ear check, Dr. Pharaoh pressed his icy stethoscope to my chest. When I inhaled and coughed, his dapper demeanor immediately grew sober. My thermometer read 103 degrees. You could fry an egg on my forehead. When he lifted up my little cotton gown, my tummy was covered with red blotches. Mom assumed I had contracted a routine case of measles, but my measles were not German and my pox was not chicken. Dr. Pharaoh concluded that I had contracted a roaring case of scarlet fever and pneumonia. Our house was quarantined, and I was confined to bed.

Mom assumed this was going to be a routine kid visit to the doctor. Instead, Dr. Pharaoh gave her a long list of prescriptions and recommended I receive a series of *gamma globulin* shots over the next three months. A yearly vaccine was one thing, but a series of shots? No way. My fate was sealed and my torture was imminent.

Physicians knew how to play "good cop, bad cop." The docs got to be chummy with all their little patients, and the nurses did all the stabbing. Nurse Sears was definitely a hottie. She sported a form-fitting white dress, white nylons, and white leather wedges. Nurses in my day dressed for their job, not like the nurses today who schlub around in Hawaiian-print scrubs and frayed-white *Keds*. Nurse Sears's perfectly-coiffed French twist was glamorously poised at the nape of her neck. She had the same line for every trembling patient perched on the examining table. "This will hurt me more than it does you," she said. Liar! That little comment was code for, "You're not going to be a cry-baby when I poke you with this needle, are you?"

I made no promises. She didn't fool me. I knew the drill. The *Bugs Bunny* bandage strip and the green lollipop didn't make it all better. A shot was a shot. I had a drawer full of lollipops and *Tootsie* rolls, and I would trade them all in for one less inoculation.

As the fall turned into winter, my condition worsened. I was really, really, really sick. My mom stayed home from work to bathe my forehead with cold washcloths and to rock me as I sobbed. At night, she clutched me to her chest while I gasped for air, but then she dropped off to sleep. I lay awake listening to *Moon River* on the radio, trying to make my heaving chest match the slow, undulating rhythm of the music. When I visited the doctor in the weeks to follow, he would shake his head and give me another shot in the bottom. Lollipops were not adequate compensation for a stinging poke down "where the sun don't shine." At that point, I was too ill to care.

Green Jeans was gone, my friends couldn't visit me because our house was off limits, and I dreaded the lonely nights of wheezing and coughing. My annoying little sister stayed at Grandma's to avoid "the plague," and Mrs. Richardson, my nanny, also kept her distance as much as possible. Weeks turned into months. I coughed through Christmas, I whined through January, and by February I had given up hope of being an Eager Beaver again.

Had God forgotten me? I couldn't even go outside and smell the fresh air. I was a prisoner in my own house. *Chutes and Ladders* played alone is just *Chutes*. Shoot! I'll bet the Eager Beavers didn't recall that I existed. The doc said I was improving and might be able to return to kindergarten in March. But four more weeks at home seemed like an eternity. I had been sentenced to solitary confinement by this evil disease. I begged for a puppy, but Mom said that furry creatures might make me wheeze.

On a particularly frosty, gloomy morning in February, I sat in my little bedroom rocker, gazing at pictures of Hansel and Gretel that I had seen five hundred times. Although I couldn't read, I knew the story by heart and determined I'd plan a bold escape from my bedroom dungeon and leave a graham cracker-crumb trail on the sidewalk in case I needed to find my way home. At least running away would let me breathe the outside air for just a little while.

Just before I made my break, I heard a knock at the front door. It didn't sound like a grown-up knock, but a little kid's rap-tap-tap. I didn't know what to think. Had the "run-away-from-home" police gotten wind of my evil plan? Who was at the door? Was my little sis coming home? Did Dougie Scott from next door learn I was soon to be germ-free? I didn't care. I just wanted to see a friendly face from the outside world.

I peered out of the frosty window and couldn't believe my eyes. Mrs. Richardson called me to come to the front door. Tommy Tugbottom, the toughest Eager Beaver of them all, smiled a toothy grin and presented me with a box—an enormous, beautiful cardboard box covered with construction paper hearts and doilies. I had completely forgotten it was Valentine's Day. Tommy handed me the present, blushed, waved, and ran toward the pick-up truck puttering in the driveway.

What treasure would I find? Why had Tommy, of all people, courageously appeared on my doorstep? I could still smell the drying wheat paste beneath the paper doilies. I lifted the lid and gasped at its contents—a veritable treasure trove of handmade cards, Valentine candy, and an unopened box of *Hershey's Kisses*. The large letter on the top was from Mrs. Drake. "Dear Julie," she wrote, "we are so sorry you have been sick. The Eager Beavers are not eager without you. Please come back to us soon. Love, Mrs. Drake."

My heart leapt with joy. I had been missed! Card after card had messages like "Get well" or "Happy Valentine's Day" scrawled in red crayon. The girls' hearts were painstakingly neat with paper doilies and taped-on candy hearts. The boys' notes were rattier, but they still managed to say something kind like "Stop sniffing . . . start living" or "Get well, Stupid."

I never felt so valued. It didn't matter that Mrs. Drake had probably threatened them within an inch of their lives if they didn't complete the assignment. I couldn't care less if Tommy and his cronies teased me when I returned. God, in His own way, had taken time to show His love for me through a few scrawny, hyperactive five-year-olds.

Mountaintops and valleys are etched in my memory, but that Valentine box was unforgettable. The despair of feeling alone and hopeless had been erased by the simple kindness of the Eager Beavers. On that misty February morning, God reminded me that I was loved, cherished, and remembered.

> *I can do everything through him who gives me strength. Yet it was good of you to share in my troubles. Moreover, as you Philippians know, in the early days of your acquaintance with the gospel, when I set out from Macedonia, not one church shared with me in the matter of giving and receiving, except you only; for even when I was in Thessalonica, you sent me aid again and again when I was in need. Not that I am looking for a gift, but I am*

looking for what may be credited to your account. I have received full payment and even more; I am amply supplied, now that I have received from Epaphroditus the gifts you sent. They are a fragrant offering, an acceptable sacrifice, pleasing to God. And my God will meet all your needs according to his glorious riches in Christ Jesus. (Philippians 4:13–19 NIV)

In this passage, we read an oft-quoted verse: "I can do all things through Christ who strengthens me" (4:13). List some difficult times you have had in your past. When have you needed God's grace the most? Did you experience God's power in those moments?

Now read verses 14–19 again. Paul not only needed God, he needed a support system to survive. What did the Philippians do for Paul?

Do you have a support system like Paul did? Who are the people in your life who come alongside you when you are hurting? List them here.

If you don't have any, ask God to bring those people into your life and consider joining a small group of Christians in your church, or a Bible study in your neighborhood. Be proactive in developing a "support team."

Grandpa Boy.

Julie age six.

Julie and Kathy.

Family Christmas 1957.

Julie trying to drink the cologne.

Julie showing off her modeling skills.

Daddy.

Mom's wedding day.

Julie's first piano recital.

Mom and Dad with their new set of wheels!

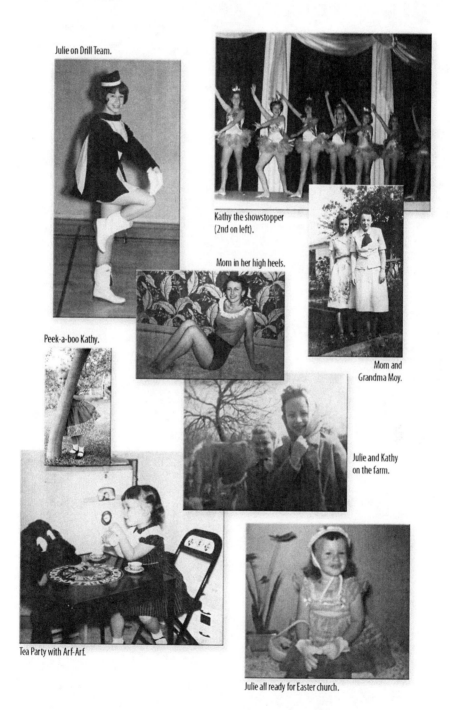

Julie on Drill Team.

Kathy the showstopper (2nd on left).

Mom in her high heels.

Peek-a-boo Kathy.

Mom and Grandma Moy.

Julie and Kathy on the farm.

Tea Party with Arf-Arf.

Julie all ready for Easter church.

231